# EVERY
# SHUT EYE
# AIN'T
# ASLEEP

AN ANTHOLOGY ■ EVERY

OF POETRY SHUT EYE

BY AFRICAN AMERICANS AIN'T

SINCE 1945 ASLEEP

■

EDITED BY
MICHAEL S. HARPER AND
ANTHONY WALTON

LITTLE, BROWN AND COMPANY

BOSTON  NEW YORK  TORONTO  LONDON

FIRST EDITION

Library of Congress Cataloging-in-Publication Data
Every shut eye ain't asleep : an anthology of poetry by African
    Americans since 1945 / edited by Michael S. Harper and Anthony Walton.
        p.    cm.
    Includes bibliographical references.
    ISBN 0-316-34712-4 (hc)
    ISBN 0-316-34710-8 (pb)
        1. American poetry — Afro-American authors. 2. American
    poetry — 20th century. 3. Afro-Americans — Poetry. I. Harper,
    Michael S. II. Walton, Anthony.
    PS591.N4E94 1994
    811'.54080896073 — dc20                                93-13500

Acknowledgments for permission to reprint material begin on page 323.

HC: 10  9  8  7  6  5  4  3  2
PB: 10  9  8  7  6  5  4  3

RRD-VA

Designed by Barbara Werden

Published simultaneously in Canada by Little, Brown & Company
(Canada) Limited

PRINTED IN THE UNITED STATES OF AMERICA

# To the Reader: Re STERLING A. BROWN

White man tells mo—hunh—
Damn yo' soul;
White man tells me—hunh—
Damn yo' soul;
Got no need, bebby,
To be tole

—"Southern Road"

*Every Shut Eye Ain't Asleep* is dedicated to the achievement of Sterling A. Brown, as a poet and folksayist, scholar-teacher, and pioneering wordsmith in a dynamic American lexicon, especially the laconic meditations and metaphysics extant in folkspeech as the underbelly of the nation's lexicon. Brown's first book of poems, *Southern Road*, was published in 1932 with an introduction by James Weldon Johnson. Brown had written an accompanying handbook to Johnson's *American Negro Poetry*, with a seminal section on prosody. The two of them, mentor and protégé, had quarreled about "dialect being limited to pathos and humor," and Brown won out because he had the better ear. What he heard was the inner discourse, rhythm, and music of a largely unlettered people with "too much" world's work life experience. Brown was not a poet of self-expression; it was the poet's duty to make the reader cry out, and in Brown's title poem to the volume, he provided a narrative to a convention, the work song, which had no tradition of story. Brown provided it. He was a believer in his people, in literary and historical tradition, and in literature as a study in how humans live and love and die. Brown was a believer in the common man, but not in common parlance. His dramatic portraits, humorous character, and regional mastery of idioms informed what he learned about his own education: "I learned the Arts and Sciences at Williams, I learned the Humanities in Lynchburg, Virginia." It was there, in Lynchburg, that he learned what he could not learn in school, the hardship of the lives of his many students—coalminers, as Brown's high school teacher Carter G. Woodson, father of Negro History Week, now Black History Month, had been a coalminer before his career as a researcher in Washington. Brown was a classical debunker in the continued assault and reduction of Black Humanity and spent much of his teaching career redressing an American tendency to stereotype the person farthest down; here Brown mined his images of endurance and fortitude. The editors wish to pay homage and heed to his abiding example regarding human standards of clarity and excellence:

> *Went down to the rocks to hide my face,*
> *The rocks cried out no hiding place.*
>
> *There's no hiding place down here.*

—MICHAEL S. HARPER
*Johannesburg/Harare*

# CONTENTS

The editors would like to thank Rosemary Cullen and the staff of the John Hay Library at Brown University for their cheerful aid and advice in using the Harris Collection, the use of an office in the Hay, and the prompt execution of various administrative and clerical tasks.

# EVERY
# SHUT EYE
# AIN'T
# ASLEEP

■

# INTRODUCTION

For African Americans, the years since World War II have been the best of times—full of joy, social progress, and affirmation—and the worst, as millions remain mired in the ghettos of the North and the rural fiefdoms of the South, fighting deathly spirals of dependency, incarceration, violence, and drug abuse. It has been a time of tumultuous change for blacks, instigated by sociological upheaval wrought by World War II itself, which caused great numbers of blacks to travel the globe, as well as the ebbing of segregation in the armed forces. Technological change—the invention of the cotton picker in the South, the relentless development of mechanized and computerized industry in the North—gave opportunity to some Americans of African descent and slammed the door in the faces of others.

This sort of brief social analysis can illuminate the last fifty years of African-American poetic practice. If poets can be said to operate within a social context—we, the editors, most surely think they can—then no group of poets is so conscious of context as are black Americans. From the first known black poet, Phillis Wheatley (1753[?]–1784), to the youngest poet included in this anthology, Elizabeth Alexander (b. 1962), each black poet has wrestled in some form with Countee Cullen's ironic conundrum:

> Yet do I marvel at the curious thing:
> To make a poet black, and bid him sing.

Cullen, his predecessor Paul Laurence Dunbar, and some of the contemporaries of both wrestled with this issue. Is a poet first a poet, or first a black? This is an underlying, if often unspoken, theme of African-American poetry since 1945, as some poets of African descent utilized the opportunities brought by social change to move into the mainstream. Others narrated the changes in their work while straddling a line between what has traditionally been thought of as the academy and what has been thought of as the black community, and still others have focused their energies and activities entirely in that community and turned their backs on the wider world. A career such as that of Rita Dove, with its uncompromised critical and commercial success and distinguished academic appointments, could only have been dreamed of by Cullen or Dunbar. Ms. Dove is able to write and, more important, publish poems as she fancies. She can deal in black folk materials, as in *Thomas and Beulah*, or she can write beautiful lyrics that are ethnically unidentifiable, and publish either in *Antæus* or in *The New Yorker*.

This is something new for black poets, as illustrated by that lament of Countee Cullen's and as emphasized by Gerald Early: "Without least depreciating the beauty of Negro Spirituals or the undeniable fact that Negro singers do them, as it were, to the manner born, we have always resented the natural inclination of most white people to demand spirituals the moment it is known that a Negro is about to sing. So often the request has seemed to savor of the feeling that we could do this and this alone."

Other younger black poets, among them Marilyn Nelson Waniek, Ai, Yusef Komunyakaa, Christopher Gilbert, Cornelius Eady, and Elizabeth Alexander, have been able to share this new possibility with Dove, along with a few pathbreakers like Jay Wright, Lucille Clifton, and Michael S. Harper. These older poets "slipped the yoke" and have had fully realized careers. But behind this success loom the specters of Dunbar, Cullen, Robert Hayden, and others who died young, were denied entry, or were not recognized until very, very late. And there are other emblematic careers: those of Gwendolyn Brooks, who achieved great success early but then seemed to withdraw into the black community; and Gloria Oden, who, forty years early, had exhibited some of the talents and ambitions of Rita Dove, but had been caught in a sort of no-man's-land between standard black practice at the time and the closed white literary world.

There was another strand of activity as well, that of the, speaking loosely, Black Arts Movement, which is represented in this book by poets like Sonia Sanchez, Amiri Baraka, and Haki Madhubuti (Don L. Lee). These poets and their artistic compatriots grew disenchanted with, and in some cases despaired of, what they saw as the reality of American culture and society and the possibility of any kind of meaningful assimilation by blacks. They instead turned exclusively to the black community for inspiration and sustenance, and took on roles as teachers and exhorters, often articulating the rage of the black masses with frightening accuracy. These poets had a tremendous vogue in the seventies, but then went into eclipse, as the trend-hopping publishing industry picked up new causes (this had also caused the demise of the Harlem, or New Negro, Renaissance) and as the movement fragmented, some members joining faculties, some becoming full-time activists and organizers, others falling into silence. And the movement was handicapped by its own success and the seductiveness of rhetoric; poets thought that they had mobilized a permanent audience, which they hadn't, and this changed what and how they wrote.

This background information allows us to address our central questions: "Why this anthology, and why now?" The necessity of this book can be seen in the contrasts between the careers of Robert Hayden and Rita Dove. How many worthwhile black artists "fell in the cracks" of mainstream recognition? In two of the taste-making anthologies of recent times, Donald Hall's *Contemporary American Poetry* and Mark Strand's *Contemporary American Poetry*, Mr. Hayden is not represented, and at most one black is featured. This is generally the case. The present volume can serve as a correction of these past oversights and as a window into the practice of one subgroup of American poets.

Another problem with the critical interpretation of black artists in the mainstream is that serious attention is often limited only to those works that are identifiably "black"—Cullen's dilemma—with "black" subject matter, themes, etc. Virtually every black poet who has written has written poems in the grand tradition of the English language—Wordsworth, Keats, Stevens—and that needs to be explored and noted as well. The tradition needs the Robert Hayden of "October," "Ice Storm," and "The Islands," as well as his "Frederick Douglass" and "Runagate Runagate." It needs the Jay Wright of "Winter," the Marilyn Waniek of "Emily Dickinson's Defunct," and the Cornelius Eady of "Crows in a Strong Wind."

There are many black voices, or more accurately, voices that can be described as "black." There has been a tendency by the academy to select a few, in the last ten years largely Messrs. Hayden, Walcott, Harper, Wright, and Ms. Dove, while overlooking Ms. Brooks, Ms. Walker, Ms. Clifton, Ms. Williams, and Mr. Eady. (Other groups of five could be chosen as well.) A goal of this anthology is to focus attention on the entire spectrum of African-American poetic practice, from the precise classicism of Gloria Oden to the vocal jazz of Jayne Cortez, while pointing toward areas of comparison and study of these various ways of writing and being American, human, and black.

The scope of the anthology is simple. Using the work and career of Robert Hayden as a kind of signpost in sensibility—call it modern, call it contemporary—poets born between 1913 and 1962, almost fifty years, three generations, have been studied and chosen by the editors. The principal qualification is quality, artistic quality in the judgment of the editors, and any oversights or omissions are theirs alone. After birth date, the other prerequisite is that the poet have published one book commercially. Space limitations, as always, made the choices difficult. How fully to feature masters like Mr. Hayden and Ms. Brooks while including as many others as possible? This led to editorial decisions that may prove controversial; time will prove the truest judge.

Many of these poems have the added attraction of their historical significance, representing a kind of social, cultural, and political narrative of America, oblique and cubist. Since the beginning blacks have been in the middle of things in America, and these poems testify to that reality and celebrate it. Blacks are "a nation within a nation," outsiders at home, and the poems allow for amazing levels of insight within short spaces, what could be called a dialectic of metaphysics and exegesis. Ralph Ellison called it "fingering the jagged grain." Literature can be thought of as a study in comparative humanity—something these poets do daily—and as a prism, in both directions, of art and what's going on in the society. When reading these poems, it is worthwhile to remember a question: Whom is the poet speaking to, and for?

The title of this volume, *Every Shut Eye Ain't Asleep*, is the first half of a couplet that concludes, "every good-bye ain't gone." This is an old folk saying from the Deep South that we feel speaks to and refracts light-years of truth about blacks and black life in America. Black poets are among those darker brothers and sisters who are often ignored, patronized, maligned, or worse. Mostly, they are unseen, working in some farther field beyond easy view. But, out of sight or not, they are there, and sometimes, they are next door, merely being quiet. This book celebrates that quiet and the culture that sustains it. It is also time to reflect upon the necessity of books like it, and to ponder the distant day when that might not be so.

MICHAEL S. HARPER
ANTHONY WALTON
*Providence, Rhode Island*
*January 1, 1994*

# ROBERT HAYDEN

## (1913–1980)

*Robert Hayden was born and raised in the Paradise Valley ghetto of Detroit, where, even as a very young man, he showed an interest in and aptitude for the library, literature, and drama. After graduating from Detroit City College, he spent time in the East, then studied for a master's degree at the University of Michigan, where his most influential teacher was W. H. Auden, who is likely responsible for much of Hayden's devotion to elegant formal construction and precise technical choice and execution. Mr. Hayden published his first book, which he would later disavow, in 1940, and over the next four decades would compile a poetic résumé that is in the very first rank of contemporary American practice. Mr. Hayden was equally comfortable in brief three- and four-line epigrams, short lyrics, and multipage, densely layered and researched epics. He was a master of vocabulary, capable of choosing words and phrases that stick in the memory and continue to startle and surprise in reading after reading. Robert Hayden's work has yet to acquire the audience or critical consideration it so richly deserves, and in later life, Mr. Hayden, with characteristic modesty, seemed to bear this oversight with equanimity. His professional life was spent as a professor, first at Fisk University, then at the University of Michigan. He died in 1980, in Ann Arbor, Michigan, of an embolism.*

## A BALLAD OF REMEMBRANCE

Quadroon mermaids, Afro angels, black saints
balanced upon the switchblades of that air
and sang. Tight streets unfolding to the eye
like fans of corrosion and elegiac lace
crackled with their singing: Shadow of time. Shadow of blood.

Shadow, echoed the Zulu king, dangling
from a cluster of balloons. Blood,
whined the gun-metal priestess, floating
over the courtyard where dead men diced.

What will you have? she inquired, the sallow vendeuse
of prepared tarnishes and jokes of nacre and ormolu,
what but those gleamings, oldrose graces,
manners like scented gloves? Contrived ghosts
rapped to metronome clack of lavalieres.

Contrived illuminations riding a threat
of river, masked Negroes wearing chameleon
satins gaudy now as a fortuneteller's
dream of disaster, lighted the crazy flopping
dance of love and hate among joys, rejections.

Accommodate, muttered the Zulu king,
toad on a throne of glaucous poison jewels.
Love, chimed the saints and the angels and the mermaids.
Hate, shrieked the gun-metal priestess
from her spiked bellcollar curved like a fleur-de-lis:

As well have a talon as a finger, a muzzle as a mouth,
as well have a hollow as a heart. And she pinwheeled
away in coruscations of laughter, scattering
those others before her like foil stars.

But the dance continued—now among metaphorical
doors, coffee cups floating poised
hysterias, decors of illusion; now among
mazurka dolls offering death's-heads
of cocaine roses and real violets.

Then you arrived, meditative, ironic,
richly human; and your presence was shore where I rested
released from the hoodoo of that dance, where I spoke
with my true voice again.

And therefore this is not only a ballad of remembrance
for the down-South arcane city with death
in its jaws like gold teeth and archaic cusswords;
not only a token for the troubled generous friends
held in the fists of that schizoid city like flowers,
but also, Mark Van Doren,
a poem of remembrance, a gift, a souvenir for you.

# THE BALLAD OF SUE ELLEN WESTERFIELD

*(for Clyde)*

She grew up in bedeviled southern wilderness,
but had not been a slave, she said,
because her father wept and set her mother free.
She hardened in perilous rivertowns
and after The Surrender,
went as maid upon the tarnished Floating Palaces.
Rivermen reviled her for the rankling cold
sardonic pride
that gave a knife-edge to her comeliness.

When she was old, her back still straight,
her hair still glossy black,
she'd talk sometimes
of dangers lived through on the rivers.
But never told of him,
whose name she'd vowed she would not speak again
till after Jordan.
Oh, he was nearer nearer now
than wearisome kith and kin.
His blue eyes followed her
as she moved about her tasks upon the *Memphis Rose*.
He smiled and joshed, his voice quickening her.
She cursed the circumstance. . . .

The crazing horrors of that summer night,
the swifting flames, he fought his way to her,
the savaging panic, and helped her swim to shore.
The steamer like besieged Atlanta blazing,
the cries, the smoke and bellowing flames,
the flamelit thrashing forms in hellmouth water,
and he swimming out to them,
leaving her dazed and lost.
A woman screaming under the raddled trees—

Sue Ellen felt it was herself who screamed.
The moaning of the hurt, the terrified—
she held off shuddering despair
and went to comfort whom she could.
Wagons torches bells
and whimpering dusk of morning
and blankness lostness nothingness for her
until his arms had lifted her
into wild and secret dark.

How long how long was it they wandered,
loving fearing loving,
fugitives whose dangerous only hidingplace
was love?
How long was it before she knew
she could not forfeit what she was,
even for him—could not, even for him,
forswear her pride?
They kissed and said farewell at last.
He wept as had her father once.
They kissed and said farewell.
Until her dying-bed,
she cursed the circumstance.

## HOMAGE TO THE EMPRESS OF THE BLUES

Because there was a man somewhere in a candystripe silk shirt,
gracile and dangerous as a jaguar and because a woman moaned
for him in sixty-watt gloom and mourned him Faithless Love
Twotiming Love Oh Love Oh Careless Aggravating Love,

> She came out on the stage in yards of pearls, emerging like
> a favorite scenic view, flashed her golden smile and sang.

Because grey laths began somewhere to show from underneath
torn hurdygurdy lithographs of dollfaced heaven;
and because there were those who feared alarming fists of snow
on the door and those who feared the riot-squad of statistics,

She came out on the stage in ostrich feathers, beaded satin,
and shone that smile on us and sang.


## THOSE WINTER SUNDAYS

Sundays too my father got up early
and put his clothes on in the blueblack cold,
then with cracked hands that ached
from labor in the weekday weather made
banked fires blaze. No one ever thanked him.

I'd wake and hear the cold splintering, breaking.
When the rooms were warm, he'd call,
and slowly I would rise and dress,
fearing the chronic angers of that house,

Speaking indifferently to him,
who had driven out the cold
and polished my good shoes as well.
What did I know, what did I know
of love's austere and lonely offices?


## RUNAGATE RUNAGATE

I.

Runs falls rises stumbles on from darkness into darkness
and the darkness thicketed with shapes of terror
and the hunters pursuing and the hounds pursuing
and the night cold and the night long and the river
to cross and the jack-muh-lanterns beckoning beckoning
and blackness ahead and when shall I reach that somewhere
morning and keep on going and never turn back and keep on going
        Runagate
              Runagate
                     Runagate

Many thousands rise and go
many thousands crossing over
                     O mythic North
                O star-shaped yonder Bible city

Some go weeping and some rejoicing
some in coffins and some in carriages
some in silks and some in shackles

      Rise and go or fare you well

No more auction block for me
no more driver's lash for me

      If you see my Pompey, 30 yrs of age,
      new breeches, plain stockings, negro shoes;
      if you see my Anna, likely young mulatto
      branded E on the right cheek, R on the left,
      catch them if you can and notify subscriber.
      Catch them if you can, but it won't be easy.
      They'll dart underground when you try to catch them,
      plunge into quicksand, whirlpools, mazes,
      turn into scorpions when you try to catch them.

And before I'll be a slave
I'll be buried in my grave

      North star and bonanza gold
      I'm bound for the freedom, freedom-bound
      and oh Susyanna don't you cry for me

          Runagate

          Runagate

    II.

Rises from their anguish and their power,

          Harriet Tubman,

          woman of earth, whipscarred,
          a summoning, a shining

          Mean to be free

And this was the way of it, brethren brethren,
way we journeyed from Can't to Can.
Moon so bright and no place to hide,
the cry up and the patterollers riding,
hound dogs belling in bladed air.
And fear starts a-murbling, Never make it,
we'll never make it. *Hush that now,*
and she's turned upon us, levelled pistol
glinting in the moonlight:
Dead folks can't jaybird-talk, she says;
you keep on going now or die, she says.

Wanted    Harriet Tubman    Alias The General
alias Moses    Stealer of Slaves
In league with Garrison    Alcott    Emerson
Garrett    Douglass    Thoreau    John Brown

Armed and known to be Dangerous

Wanted    Reward    Dead or Alive

     Tell me, Ezekiel, oh tell me do you see
     mailed Jehovah coming to deliver me?

Hoot-owl calling in the ghosted air,
five times calling to the hants in the air.
Shadow of a face in the scary leaves,
shadow of a voice in the talking leaves:

     Come ride-a my train

     *Oh that train, ghost-story train*
     *through swamp and savanna movering movering,*
     *over trestles of dew, through caves of the wish,*
     *Midnight Special on a sabre track movering movering,*
     *first stop Mercy and the last Hallelujah.*

     Come ride-a my train

     Mean mean mean to be free.

## FREDERICK DOUGLASS

When it is finally ours, this freedom, this liberty, this beautiful
and terrible thing, needful to man as air,
usable as earth; when it belongs at last to all,
when it is truly instinct, brain matter, diastole, systole,
reflex action; when it is finally won; when it is more
than the gaudy mumbo jumbo of politicians:
this man, this Douglass, this former slave, this Negro
beaten to his knees, exiled, visioning a world
where none is lonely, none hunted, alien,
this man, superb in love and logic, this man
shall be remembered. Oh, not with statues' rhetoric,
not with legends and poems and wreaths of bronze alone,
but with the lives grown out of his life, the lives
fleshing his dream of the beautiful, needful thing.

## The Dream
(1863)

That evening Sinda thought she heard the drums
and hobbled from her cabin to the yard.
The quarters now were lonely-still in willow dusk
after the morning's ragged jubilo,
when laughing crying singing the folks went off
with Marse Lincum's soldier boys.
But Sinda hiding would not follow them: those
Buckras with their ornery
funning, cussed commands, oh they were not were not
the hosts the dream had promised her.

and hope when these few lines reaches your hand they
will fine you well. I am tired some but it is war you know
and ole Jeff Davis muss be ketch an hung to a sour apple
tree like it says in the song    I seen some akshun but
that is what i listed for not to see the sights ha ha More of
our peeples coming every day. the Kernul calls them
contrybans and has them work aroun the Camp and
learning to be soljurs. How is the wether home. Its warm
this evening but theres been lots of rain

How many times that dream had come to her—
more vision than a dream—
    the great big soldiers marching out of gunburst,
their faces those of Cal and Joe
    and Charlie sold to the ricefields oh sold away
a-many and a-many a long year ago.
    Fevered, gasping, Sinda listened, knew this was
the ending of her dream and prayed
    that death, grown fretful and impatient, nagging her,
would wait a little longer, would let her see.


    and we been marching sleeping too in cold rain and
mirey mud a heap a times. Tell Mama Thanks for The
Bible an not worry so. Did brother fix the roof yet like
he promised? this mus of been a real nice place befor the
fighting uglied it all up the judas trees is blosommed out
so pretty same as if this hurt and truble wasnt going on.
Almos like somthing you mite dream about i take it for
a sign The Lord remembers Us Theres talk we will be
moving into Battle very soon agin


    Trembling tottering Hep me Jesus Sinda crossed
the wavering yard, reached
    a redbud tree in bloom, could go no farther, clung
to the bole and clinging fell
    to her knees. She tried to stand, could not so much
as lift her head, tried to hold
    the bannering sounds, heard only the whippoorwills
in tenuous moonlight; struggled to rise
    and make her way to the road to welcome Joe and Cal
and Charlie, fought with brittle strength to rise.


    So pray for me that if the Bullit with my name rote on
it get me it will not get me in retreet i do not think them
kine of thots so much no need in Dying till you die I all
ways figger, coursc if the hardtack and the bullybeef do
not kill me nuthing can i guess. Tell Joe I hav shure
seen me some ficety gals down here in Dixieland & i
mite jus go ahead an jump over the broomstick with one
and bring her home, well I muss close with Love to all
& hope to see you soon Yrs Cal

# EL-HAJJ MALIK EL-SHABAZZ

(Malcolm X)

O masks and metamorphoses of Ahab, Native Son

### I

The icy evil that struck his father down
and ravished his mother into madness
trapped him in violence of a punished self
struggling to break free.

As Home Boy, as Dee-troit Red,
he fled his name, became the quarry of
his own obsessed pursuit.

He conked his hair and Lindy-hopped,
zoot-suited jiver, swinging those chicks
in the hot rose and reefer glow.

His injured childhood bullied him.
He skirmished in the Upas trees
and cannibal flowers of the American Dream—

but could not hurt the enemy
powered against him there.

### II

Sometimes the dark that gave his life
its cold satanic sheen would shift
a little, and he saw himself
floodlit and eloquent;

yet how could he, "Satan" in The Hole,
guess what the waking dream foretold?

Then false dawn of vision came;
he fell upon his face before
a racist Allah pledged to wrest him from
the hellward-thrusting hands of Calvin's Christ—

to free him and his kind
from Yakub's white-faced treachery.
He rose redeemed from all but prideful anger,

though adulterate attars could not cleanse
him of the odors of the pit.

III

*Asalam alaikum!*

He X'd his name, became his people's anger,
exhorted them to vengeance for their past;
rebuked, admonished them,

their scourger who
would shame them, drive them from
the lush ice gardens of their servitude.

*Asalam alaikum!*

Rejecting Ahab, he was of Ahab's tribe.
"Strike through the mask!"

IV

Time. "The martyr's time," he said.
Time and the karate killer,
knifer, gunman. Time that brought
ironic trophies as his faith

twined sparking round the bole,
the fruit of neo-Islam.
"The martyr's time."

But first, the ebb time pilgrimage
toward revelation, hejira to
his final metamorphosis;

*Labbayk! Labbayk!*

He fell upon his face before
Allah the raceless in whose blazing Oneness all
were one. He rose renewed renamed, became
much more than there was time for him to be.

# OCTOBER

### I

October—
its plangency, its glow

as of words in
the poet's mind,

as of God in
the saint's.

### II

I wept for your mother
in her pain, wept in
my joy when you were
born,
     Maia,
that October morning.
We named you
for a star a star-like
poem sang.
       I write this
for your birthday
and say I love you
and say October
like the phoenix sings you.

### III

This chiming
and tolling
    of lion
and phoenix
and chimera
    colors.
This huntsman's
horn, sounding
    mort for
quarry fleeing
through mirrors
    of burning
into deathless
    dying.

IV

Rockweight
of surprising snow

crushed
the October trees,

broke
branches that

crashing set
the snow on fire.


## A PLAGUE OF STARLINGS
(Fisk Campus)

Evenings I hear
the workmen fire
into the stiff
magnolia leaves,
routing the starlings
gathered noisy and
befouling there.

Their scissoring
terror like glass
coins spilling breaking
the birds explode
into mica sky
raggedly fall
to ground rigid
in clench of cold.

The spared return,
when the guns are through,
to the spoiled trees
like choiceless poor
to a dangerous
dwelling place,
chitter and quarrel
in the piercing dark
above the killed.

Mornings, I pick
my way past death's
black droppings:
on campus lawns
and streets
the troublesome
starlings
frost-salted lie,
troublesome still.

And if not careful
I shall tread
upon carcasses
carcasses when I
go mornings now
to lecture on
what Socrates,
the hemlock hour nigh,
told sorrowing
Phaedo and the rest
about the migratory
habits of the soul.


## THE NIGHT-BLOOMING CEREUS

And so for nights
we waited, hoping to see
the heavy bud
break into flower.

On its neck-like tube
hooking down from the edge
of the leaf-branch
    nearly to the floor,

    the bud packed
tight with its miracle swayed
stiffly on breaths
    of air, moved

    as though impelled
by stirrings within itself.
It repelled as much
    as it fascinated me

    sometimes—snake,
eyeless bird head,
beak that would gape
    with grotesque life-squawk.

    But you, my dear,
conceded less to the bizarre
than to the imminence
    of bloom. Yet we agreed

    we ought
to celebrate the blossom,
paint ourselves, dance
    in honor of

    archaic mysteries
when it appeared. Meanwhile
we waited, aware
    of rigorous design.

    Backster's
polygraph, I thought,
would have shown
    (as clearly as it had

    a philodendron's
fear) tribal sentience
in the cactus, focused
    energy of will.

That belling of
tropic perfume—that
signalling
        not meant for us;

        the darkness
cloyed with summoning
fragrance. We dropped
        trivial tasks

        and marvelling
beheld at last the achieved
flower. Its moonlight
        petals were

        still unfold-
ing, the spike fringe of the outer
perianth recessing
        as we watched.

        Lunar presence,
foredoomed, already dying,
it charged the room
        with plangency

        older than human
cries, ancient as prayers
invoking Osiris, Krishna,
        Tezcátlipóca.

        We spoke
in whispers when
we spoke
        at all . . .

# FREE FANTASIA: TIGER FLOWERS

*(for Michael)*

The sporting people
along St. Antoine—
that scufflers'
paradise of ironies—
        bet salty money
on his righteous
        hook and jab.

I was a boy then, running
(unbeknownst to Pa)
errands for Miss Jackie
and Stack-o'-Diamonds' Eula Mae.
. . . Their perfumes,
rouged Egyptian faces.
        Their pianolas jazzing.

O Creole babies,
Dixie odalisques,
speeding through cutglass
dark to see the macho angel
        trick you'd never
turn, his bluesteel prowess
        in the ring.

Hardshell believers
amen'd the wreck
as God A'mighty's
will. I'd thought
        such gaiety could not
die. Nor could our
        elegant avenger.

*The Virgin Forest*
by Rousseau—
its psychedelic flowers
towering, its deathless
        dark dream figure

death the leopard
       claws—I choose it
now as elegy
       for Tiger Flowers.


## A LETTER FROM PHILLIS WHEATLEY
London, 1773

Dear Obour
              Our crossing was without
event. I could not help, at times,
reflecting on that first—my Destined—
voyage long ago (I yet
have some remembrance of its Horrors)
and marvelling at God's Ways.
       Last evening, her Ladyship presented me
to her illustrious Friends.
I scarce could tell them anything
of Africa, though much of Boston
and my hope of Heaven. I read
my latest Elegies to them.
"O Sable Muse!" the Countess cried,
embracing me, when I had done.
I held back tears, as is my wont,
and there were tears in Dear
Nathaniel's eyes.
       At supper—I dined apart
like captive Royalty—
the Countess and her Guests promised
signatures affirming me
True Poetess, albeit once a slave.
Indeed, they were most kind, and spoke,
moreover, of presenting me
at Court (I thought of Pocahontas)—
an Honor, to be sure, but one,
I should, no doubt, as Patriot decline.
       My health is much improved;
I feel I may, if God so Wills,
entirely recover here.
Idyllic England! Alas, there is
no Eden without its Serpent. Under
the chiming Complaisance I hear him Hiss;

I see his flickering tongue
when foppish would-be Wits
murmur of the Yankee Pedlar
and his Cannibal Mockingbird.
      Sister, forgive th'intrusion of
my Sombreness—Nocturnal Mood
I would not share with any save
your trusted Self. Let me disperse,
in closing, such unseemly Gloom
by mention of an Incident
you may, as I, consider Droll:
Today, a little Chimney Sweep,
his face and hands with soot quite Black,
staring hard at me, politely asked:
"Does you, M'lady, sweep chimneys too?"
I was amused, but dear Nathaniel
(ever Solicitous) was not.
      I pray the Blessings of our Lord
and Saviour Jesus Christ be yours
Abundantly. In His Name,

                         Phillis


## CRISPUS ATTUCKS

Name in a footnote. Faceless name.
Moot hero shrouded in Betsy Ross
and Garvey flags—propped up
by bayonets, forever falling.


## PAUL LAURENCE DUNBAR

                *(for Herbert Martin)*

      We lay red roses on his grave,
speak sorrowfully of him
as if he were but newly dead

And so it seems to us
this raw spring day, though years
before we two were born he was
     a young poet dead.

     Poet of our youth—
his "cri du coeur" our own,
his verses "in a broken tongue"

     beguiling as an elder
brother's antic lore.
Their sad blackface lilt and croon
     survive him like

     The happy look (subliminal
of victim, dying man)
a summer's tintypes hold.

     The roses flutter in the wind;
we weight their stems
with stones, then drive away.


## ICE STORM

Unable to sleep, or pray, I stand
by the window looking out
at moonstruck trees a December storm
has bowed with ice.

Maple and mountain ash bend
under its glassy weight,
their cracked branches falling upon
the frozen snow.

The trees themselves, as in winters past,
will survive their burdening,
broken thrive. And am I less to You,
my God, than they?

## THE POINT

(Stonington, Connecticut)

Land's end. And sound and river come
together, flowing to the sea.
Wild swans, the first I've ever seen,
cross the Point in translucent flight.
On lowtide rocks terns gather;
sunbathers gather on the lambent shore.

All for a moment seems inscribed
on brightness, as on sunlit
bronze and stone, here at land's end,
praise for dead patriots of Stonington;
we are for an instant held in shining
like memories in the mind of God.


## THE ISLANDS

*(for Steve and Nancy, Allen and Magda)*

Always this waking dream of palmtrees,
magic flowers—of sensual joys
like treasures brought up from the sea.

Always this longing, this nostalgia
for tropic islands we
have never known and yet recall.

We look for ease upon these islands named
to honor holiness; in their chromatic
torpor catch our breath.

Scorn greets us with promises of rum,
hostility welcomes us to bargain sales.
We make friends with Flamboyant trees.

Jamaican Cynthie, called alien by dese lazy
islanders—wo'k hahd, treated bad,
oh, mahn, I tellin you. She's full

of raucous anger. Nevertheless brings gifts of
scarlet hibiscus when she comes to clean,
white fragrant spider-lilies too sometimes.

The roofless walls, the tidy ruins
of a sugar mill. More than cane
was crushed. But I am tired today

of history, its patina'd cliches
of endless evil. Flame trees.
The intricate sheen of waters flowing into sun.

I wake and see
the morning like a god
in peacock-flower mantle dancing

on opalescent waves—
and can believe my furies have
abandoned for a time their long pursuit.


## ASTRONAUTS

Armored in oxygen,
        faceless in visors—
mirrormasks reflecting
        the mineral glare and
shadow of moonscape—
        they walk slowmotion
floatingly the lifeless
        dust of Taurus
Littrow. And Wow, they
        exclaim; oh boy, this is it.

        They sing, exulting
(though trained to be wary
        of "emotion and
philosophy"), breaking
        the calcined stillness
of once Absolute Otherwhere.

Risking edges, earthlings
		to whom only
their machines are friendly
		(and God's radar-
watching eye?), they
		labor at gathering
proof of hypothesis;
		in snowshine of sunlight
dangerous as radium
		probe detritus for clues.

		What is it we wish them
to find for us, as
		we watch them on our
screens? They loom there
		heroic antiheroes,
smaller than myth and
		poignantly human.
Why are we troubled?
		What do we ask of these men?
What do we ask of ourselves?


## [AMERICAN JOURNAL]

here among them   the americans   this baffling
multi people   extremes and variegations   their
noise   restlessness   their almost frightening
energy   how best describe these aliens in my
reports to The Counselors

disguise myself in order to study them unobserved
adapting their varied pigmentations   white black
red brown yellow   the imprecise and strangering
distinctions by which they live   by which they
justify their cruelties to one another

charming savages   enlightened primitives   brash
new comers lately sprung up in our galaxy   how
describe them   do they indeed know what or who
they are   do not seem to   yet no other beings
in the universe make more extravagant claims
for their importance and identity

like us they have created a veritable populace
of machines that serve and soothe and pamper
and entertain    we have seen their flags and
foot prints on the moon    also the intricate
rubbish left behind    a wastefully ingenious
people    many it appears worship the Unknowable
Essence    the same for them as for us    but are
more faithful to their machine made gods
technologists their shamans


oceans deserts mountains grain fields canyons
forests    variousness of landscapes weathers
sun light moon light as at home    much here is
beautiful    dream like vistas reminding me of
home    item    have seen the rock place known
as garden of the gods and sacred to the first
indigenes    red monoliths of home    despite
the tensions i breathe in i am attracted to
the vigorous americans    disturbing sensuous
appeal of so many    never to be admitted


something they call the american dream    sure
we still believe in it i guess    an earth man
in the tavern said    irregardless of the some
times night mare facts we always try to double
talk our way around    and its okay the dreams
okay and means whats good could be a damn sight
better    means every body in the good old u s a
should have the chance to get ahead or at least
should have three squares a day    as for myself
i do okay    not crying hunger with a loaf of
bread tucked under my arm you understand    i
fear one does not clearly follow i replied
notice you got a funny accent pal    like where
you from he asked    far from here i mumbled
he stared hard    i left


must be more careful    item    learn to use okay
their pass word    okay

crowds gathering in the streets today for some
reason obscure to me    noise and violent motion
repulsive physical contact    sentinels    pigs
i heard them called    with flailing clubs    rage
and bleeding and frenzy and screaming    machines
wailing    unbearable decibels    i fled lest
vibrations of the brutal scene do further harm
to my metabolism already over taxed

The Counselors would never permit such barbarous
confusion    they know what is best for our sereni
ty    we are an ancient race and have outgrown
illusions cherished here    item    their vaunted
liberty    no body pushes me around i have heard
them say    land of the free they sing    what do
they fear mistrust betray more than the freedom
they boast of in their ignorant pride    have seen
the squalid ghettoes in their violent cities
paradox on paradox    how have the americans
managed to survive

parades fireworks displays video spectacles
much grandiloquence much buying and selling
they are celebrating their history    earth men
in antique uniforms play at the carnage whereby
the americans achieved identity    we too recall
that struggle as enterprise of suffering and
faith uniquely theirs    blonde miss teen age
america waving from a red white and blue flower
float as the goddess of liberty    a divided
people seeking reassurance from a past few under
stand and many scorn    why should we sanction
old hypocrisies    thus dissenters    The Counse
lors would silence them

a decadent people The Counselors believe    i
do not find them decadent    a refutation not
permitted me    but for all their knowledge
power and inventiveness not yet more than raw
crude neophytes like earthlings everywhere

though i have easily passed for an american    in
bankers grey afro and dashiki long hair and jeans
hard hat yarmulke mini skirt    describe in some
detail for the amusement of The Counselors    and
though my skill in mimicry is impeccable    as
indeed The Counselors are aware    some thing
eludes me    some constant amid the variables
defies analysis and imitation    will i be judged
incompetent

america    as much a problem in metaphysics as
it is a nation earthly entity an iota in our
galaxy    an organism that changes even as i
examine it    fact and fantasy never twice the
same    so many variables

exert greater caution    twice have aroused
suspicion    returned to the ship until rumors
of humanoids from outer space    so their scoff
ing media voices termed us    had been laughed
away    my crew and i laughed too of course

confess i am curiously drawn    unmentionable    to
the americans    doubt i could exist among them for
long however    psychic demands far too severe
much violence    much that repels    i am attracted
none the less    their variousness their ingenuity
their elan vital    and that some thing    essence
quiddity    i cannot penetrate or name

■

# GWENDOLYN BROOKS

## (B. 1917)

*Born in Topeka, Kansas, Gwendolyn Brooks grew up in Chicago, at-
tending school and college there, and published her first book of
poems in 1945,* A Street in Bronzeville *(Bronzeville is her career-long
appellation for Black Chicago). In 1950, her book* Annie Allen *won
the Pulitzer Prize, and she has garnered numerous awards and honors*

*since, including the Poet Laureateship of the state of Illinois. Her poems, while revealing a wide span of influences ranging from Dickinson, Robinson, and Frost to Dunbar, Cullen, and Melvin Tolson, are strangely and completely her own, a unique accomplishment in American letters and one of the enduring poetic edifices of this time. Taken as a whole, Ms. Brooks's poems represent a long novel of the experiences of African Americans in Chicago, Russian in scope, emotion, and complexity, American and modern, even cubist at times, in their compression and technical wizardry. Gwendolyn Brooks is the author of nearly thirty books, including a novel,* Maud Martha, *and an autobiography,* Report from Part One. *She lives in Chicago.*

## THE MOTHER

Abortions will not let you forget.
You remember the children you got that you did not get,
The damp small pulps with a little or with no hair,
The singers and workers that never handled the air.
You will never neglect or beat
Them, or silence or buy with a sweet.
You will never wind up the sucking-thumb
Or scuttle off ghosts that come.
You will never leave them, controlling your luscious sigh,
Return for a snack of them, with gobbling mother-eye.

I have heard in the voices of the wind the voices of my dim killed
      children.
I have contracted. I have eased
My dim dears at the breasts they could never suck.
I have said, Sweets, if I sinned, if I seized
Your luck
And your lives from your unfinished reach,
If I stole your births and your names,
Your straight baby tears and your games,
Your stilted or lovely loves, your tumults, your marriages, aches, and
      your deaths,
If I poisoned the beginnings of your breaths,
Believe that even in my deliberateness I was not deliberate.
Though why should I whine,
Whine that the crime was other than mine? —
Since anyhow you are dead.

Or rather, or instead,
You were never made.
But that too, I am afraid,
Is faulty: oh, what shall I say, how is the truth to be said?
You were born, you had body, you died.
It is just that you never giggled or planned or cried.

Believe me, I loved you all.
Believe me, I knew you, though faintly, and I loved, I loved you
All.

## A SONG IN THE FRONT YARD

I've stayed in the front yard all my life.
I want a peek at the back
Where it's rough and untended and hungry weed grows.
A girl gets sick of a rose.

I want to go in the back yard now
And maybe down the alley,
To where the charity children play.
I want a good time today.

They do some wonderful things.
They have some wonderful fun.
My mother sneers, but I say it's fine
How they don't have to go in at quarter to nine.
My mother, she tells me that Johnnie Mae
Will grow up to be a bad woman.
That George'll be taken to Jail soon or late
(On account of last winter he sold our back gate).

But I say it's fine. Honest, I do.
And I'd like to be a bad woman, too,
And wear the brave stockings of night-black lace
And strut down the streets with paint on my face.

## SADIE AND MAUD

Maud went to college.
Sadie stayed at home.
Sadie scraped life
With a fine-tooth comb.

She didn't leave a tangle in.
Her comb found every strand.
Sadie was one of the livingest chits
In all the land.

Sadie bore two babies
Under her maiden name.
Maud and Ma and Papa
Nearly died of shame.
Every one but Sadie
Nearly died of shame.

When Sadie said her last so-long
Her girls struck out from home.
(Sadie had left as heritage
Her fine-tooth comb.)

Maud, who went to college,
Is a thin brown mouse.
She is living all alone
In this old house.


## OF DE WITT WILLIAMS ON HIS WAY TO LINCOLN CEMETERY

He was born in Alabama.
He was bred in Illinois.
He was nothing but a
Plain black boy.

Swing low swing low sweet sweet chariot.
Nothing but a plain black boy.

Drive him past the Pool Hall.
Drive him past the Show.
Blind within his casket,
But maybe he will know.

Down through Forty-seventh Street:
Underneath the L,
And—Northwest Corner, Prairie,
That he loved so well.

Don't forget the Dance Halls—
Warwick and Savoy,
Where he picked his women, where
He drank his liquid joy.

Born in Alabama.
Bred in Illinois.
He was nothing but a
Plain black boy.

Swing low swing low sweet sweet chariot.
Nothing but a plain black boy.


## PIANO AFTER WAR

On a snug evening I shall watch her fingers,
Cleverly ringed, declining to clever pink,
Beg glory from the willing keys. Old hungers
Will break their coffins, rise to eat and thank.
And music, warily, like the golden rose
That sometimes after sunset warms the west,
Will warm that room, persuasively suffuse
That room and me, rejuvenate a past.
But suddenly, across my climbing fever
Of proud delight—a multiplying cry.
A cry of bitter dead men who will never
Attend a gentle maker of musical joy.
Then my thawed eye will go again to ice.
And stone will shove the softness from my face.

## MENTORS

For I am rightful fellow of their band.
My best allegiances are to the dead.
I swear to keep the dead upon my mind,
Disdain for all time to be overglad.
Among spring flowers, under summer trees,
By chilling autumn waters, in the frosts
Of supercilious winter—all my days
I'll have as mentors those reproving ghosts.
And at that cry, at that remotest whisper,
I'll stop my casual business. Leave the banquet.
Or leave the ball—reluctant to unclasp her
Who may be fragrant as the flower she wears,
Make gallant bows and dim excuses, then quit
Light for the midnight that is mine and theirs.


## BEVERLY HILLS, CHICAGO

("and the people live till they have white hair")
E. M. Price

The dry brown coughing beneath their feet,
(Only a while, for the handyman is on his way)
These people walk their golden gardens.
We say ourselves fortunate to be driving by today.

That we may look at them, in their gardens where
The summer ripeness rots. But not raggedly.
Even the leaves fall down in lovelier patterns here.
And the refuse, the refuse is a neat brilliancy.

When they flow sweetly into their houses
With softness and slowness touched by that everlasting gold,
We know what they go to. To tea. But that does not mean
They will throw some little black dots into some water and add sugar
        and the juice of the cheapest lemons that are sold,

While downstairs that woman's vague phonograph bleats, "Knock me
    a kiss."
And the living all to be made again in the sweatingest physical
    manner
Tomorrow. . . . Not that anybody is saying that these people have no
    trouble.
Merely that it is trouble with a gold-flecked beautiful banner.

Nobody is saying that these people do not ultimately cease to be. And
Sometimes their passings are even more painful than ours.
It is just that so often they live till their hair is white.
They make excellent corpses, among the expensive flowers. . . .

Nobody is furious. Nobody hates these people.
At least, nobody driving by in this car.
It is only natural, however, that it should occur to us
How much more fortunate they are than we are.

It is only natural that we should look and look
At their wood and brick and stone
And think, while a breath of pine blows,
How different these are from our own.

We do not want them to have less.
But it is only natural that we should think we have not enough.
We drive on, we drive on.
When we speak to each other our voices are a little gruff.


## THE BEAN EATERS

They eat beans mostly, this old yellow pair.
Dinner is a casual affair.
Plain chipware on a plain and creaking wood,
Tin flatware.

Two who are Mostly Good.
Two who have lived their day,
But keep on putting on their clothes
And putting things away.

And remembering . . .
Remembering, with twinklings and twinges,
As they lean over the beans in their rented back room that
      is full of beads and receipts and dolls and cloths,
      tobacco crumbs, vases and fringes.


## WE REAL COOL

> THE POOL PLAYERS.
> SEVEN AT THE GOLDEN SHOVEL.

We real cool. We
Left school. We

Lurk late. We
Strike straight. We

Sing sin. We
Thin gin. We

Jazz June. We
Die soon.


## A BRONZEVILLE MOTHER LOITERS IN MISSISSIPPI. MEANWHILE, A MISSISSIPPI MOTHER BURNS BACON.

From the first it had been like a
Ballad. It had the beat inevitable. It had the blood.
A wildness cut up, and tied in little bunches,
Like the four-line stanzas of the ballads she had never quite
Understood—the ballads they had set her to, in school.

Herself: the milk-white maid, the "maid mild"
Of the ballad. Pursued
By the Dark Villain. Rescued by the Fine Prince.
The Happiness-Ever-After.
That was worth anything.
It was good to be a "maid mild."
That made the breath go fast.

Her bacon burned. She
Hastened to hide it in the step-on can, and
Drew more strips from the meat case. The eggs and sour-milk biscuits
Did well. She set out a jar
Of her new quince preserve.

. . . But there was a something about the matter of the Dark Villain.
He should have been older, perhaps.
The hacking down of a villain was more fun to think about
When his menace possessed undisputed breadth, undisputed height,
And a harsh kind of vice.
And best of all, when his history was cluttered
With the bones of many eaten knights and princesses.

The fun was disturbed, then all but nullified
When the Dark Villain was a blackish child
Of fourteen, with eyes still too young to be dirty,
And a mouth too young to have lost every reminder
Of its infant softness.

That boy must have been surprised! For
These were grown-ups. Grown-ups were supposed to be wise.
And the Fine Prince—and that other—so tall, so broad, so
Grown! Perhaps the boy had never guessed
That the trouble with grown-ups was that under the magnificent shell
        of adulthood, just under,
Waited the baby full of tantrums.
It occurred to her that there may have been something
Ridiculous in the picture of the Fine Prince
Rushing (rich with the breadth and height and
Mature solidness whose lack, in the Dark Villain, was impressing her,
Confronting her more and more as this first day after the trial
And acquittal wore on) rushing
With his heavy companion to hack down (unhorsed)
That little foe.
So much had happened, she could not remember now what that foe
        had done
Against her, or if anything had been done.
The one thing in the world that she did know and knew
With terrifying clarity was that her composition
Had disintegrated. That, although the pattern prevailed,
The breaks were everywhere. That she could think
Of no thread capable of the necessary
Sew-work.

She made the babies sit in their places at the table.
Then, before calling Him, she hurried
To the mirror with her comb and lipstick. It was necessary
To be more beautiful than ever.
The beautiful wife.
For sometimes she fancied he looked at her as though
Measuring her. As if he considered, Had she been worth It?
Had *she* been worth the blood, the cramped cries, the little stuttering
    bravado,
The gradual dulling of those Negro eyes,
The sudden, overwhelming *little-boyness* in that barn?
Whatever she might feel or half-feel, the lipstick necessity was
    something apart. He must never conclude
That she had not been worth It.

He sat down, the Fine Prince, and
Began buttering a biscuit. He looked at his hands.
He twisted in his chair, he scratched his nose.
He glanced again, almost secretly, at his hands.
More papers were in from the North, he mumbled. More meddling
    headlines.
With their pepper-words, "bestiality," and "barbarism," and
"Shocking."
The half-sneers he had mastered for the trial worked across
His sweet and pretty face.

What he'd like to do, he explained, was kill them all.
The time lost. The unwanted fame.
Still, it had been fun to show those intruders
A thing or two. To show that snappy-eyed mother,
That sassy, Northern, brown-black—

Nothing could stop Mississippi.
He knew that. Big Fella
Knew that.
And, what was so good, Mississippi knew that.
Nothing and nothing could stop Mississippi.
They could send in their petitions, and scar
Their newspapers with bleeding headlines. Their governors
Could appeal to Washington . . .

"What I want," the older baby said, "is 'lasses on my jam."
Whereupon the younger baby
Picked up the molasses pitcher and threw
The molasses in his brother's face. Instantly
The Fine Prince leaned across the table and slapped
The small and smiling criminal.

She did not speak. When the Hand
Came down and away, and she could look at her child,
At her baby-child,
She could think only of blood.
Surely her baby's cheek
Had disappeared, and in its place, surely,
Hung a heaviness, a lengthening red, a red that had no end.
She shook her head. It was not true, of course.
It was not true at all. The
Child's face was as always, the
Color of the paste in her paste-jar.

She left the table, to the tune of the children's lamentations, which
        were shriller
Than ever. She
Looked out of a window. She said not a word. *That*
Was one of the new Somethings—
The fear,
Tying her as with iron.

Suddenly she felt his hands upon her. He had followed her
To the window. The children were whimpering now.
Such bits of tots. And she, their mother,
Could not protect them. She looked at her shoulders, still
Gripped in the claim of his hands. She tried, but could not resist the
        idea
That a red ooze was seeping, spreading darkly, thickly, slowly,
Over her white shoulders, her own shoulders,
And over all of Earth and Mars.

He whispered something to her, did the Fine Prince, something
About love, something about love and night and intention.
She heard no hoof-beat of the horse and saw no flash of the shining
        steel.

He pulled her face around to meet
His, and there it was, close close,
For the first time in all those days and nights.
His mouth, wet and red,
So very, very, very red,
Closed over hers.

Then a sickness heaved within her. The courtroom Coca-Cola,
The courtroom beer and hate and sweat and drone,
Pushed like a wall against her. She wanted to bear it.
But his mouth would not go away and neither would the
Decapitated exclamation points in that Other Woman's eyes.

She did not scream.
She stood there.
But a hatred for him burst into glorious flower,
And its perfume enclasped them—big,
Bigger than all magnolias.

The last bleak news of the ballad.
The rest of the rugged music.
The last quatrain.


## THE LAST QUATRAIN OF THE
## BALLAD OF EMMETT TILL

AFTER THE MURDER,
AFTER THE BURIAL

Emmett's mother is a pretty-faced thing;
        the tint of pulled taffy.
She sits in a red room,
        drinking black coffee.
She kisses her killed boy.
        And she is sorry.
Chaos in windy grays
        through a red prairie.

# THE LOVERS OF THE POOR

   arrive. The Ladies from the Ladies' Betterment
 League
Arrive in the afternoon, the late light slanting
In diluted gold bars across the boulevard brag
Of proud, seamed faces with mercy and murder hinting
Here, there, interrupting, all deep and debonair,
The pink paint on the innocence of fear;
Walk in a gingerly manner up the hall.
Cutting with knives served by their softest care,
Served by their love, so barbarously fair.
Whose mothers taught: You'd better not be cruel!
You had better not throw stones upon the wrens!
Herein they kiss and coddle and assault
Anew and dearly in the innocence
With which they baffle nature. Who are full,
Sleek, tender-clad, fit, fiftyish, a-glow, all
Sweetly abortive, hinting at fat fruit,
Judge it high time that fiftyish fingers felt
Beneath the lovelier planes of enterprise.
To resurrect. To moisten with milky chill.
To be a random hitching post or plush.
To be, for wet eyes, random and handy hem.
   Their guild is giving money to the poor.
The worthy poor. The very very worthy
And beautiful poor. Perhaps just not too swarthy?
Perhaps just not too dirty nor too dim
Nor—passionate. In truth, what they could wish
Is—something less than derelict or dull.
Not staunch enough to stab, though, gaze for gaze!
God shield them sharply from the beggar-bold!
The noxious needy ones whose battle's bald
Nonetheless for being voiceless, hits one down.
   But it's all so bad! and entirely too much for them.
The stench; the urine, cabbage, and dead beans,
Dead porridges of assorted dusty grains,
The old smoke, *heavy* diapers, and, they're told,
Something called chitterlings. The darkness. Drawn
Darkness, or dirty light. The soil that stirs.

The soil that looks the soil of centuries.
And for that matter the *general* oldness. Old
Wood. Old marble. Old tile. Old old old.
Not homekind Oldness! Not Lake Forest, Glencoe.
Nothing is sturdy, nothing is majestic,
There is no quiet drama, no rubbed glaze, no
Unkillable infirmity of such
A tasteful turn as lately they have left,
Glencoe, Lake Forest, and to which their cars
Must presently restore them. When they're done
With dullards and distortions of this fistic
Patience of the poor and put-upon.

      They've never seen such a make-do-ness as
Newspaper rugs before! In this, this "flat,"
Their hostess is gathering up the oozed, the rich
Rugs of the morning (tattered! the bespattered . . . ),
Readies to spread clean rugs for afternoon.
Here is a scene for you. The Ladies look,
In horror, behind a substantial citizeness
Whose trains clank out across her swollen heart.
Who, arms akimbo, almost fills a door.
All tumbling children, quilts dragged to the floor
And tortured thereover, potato peelings, soft-
Eyed kitten, hunched-up, haggard, to-be-hurt.

      Their League is allotting largesse to the Lost.
But to put their clean, their pretty money, to put
Their money collected from delicate rose-fingers
Tipped with their hundred flawless rose-nails seems . . .

      They own Spode, Lowestoft, candelabra,
Mantels, and hostess gowns, and sunburst clocks,
Turtle soup, Chippendale, red satin "hangings,"
Aubussons and Hattie Carnegie. They Winter
In Palm Beach; cross the Water in June; attend,
When suitable, the nice Art Institute;
Buy the right books in the best bindings; saunter
On Michigan, Easter mornings, in sun or wind.
Oh Squalor! This sick four-story hulk, this fibre
With fissures everywhere! Why, what are bringings
Of loathe-love largesse? What shall peril hungers
So old old, what shall flatter the desolate?

Tin can, blocked fire escape and chitterling
And swaggering seeking youth and the puzzled wreckage
Of the middle passage, and urine and stale shames
And, again, the porridges of the underslung
And children children children. Heavens! That
Was a rat, surely, off there, in the shadows? Long
And long-tailed? Gray? The Ladies from the Ladies'
Betterment League agree it will be better
To achieve the outer air that rights and steadies,
To hie to a house that does not holler, to ring
Bells elsetime, better presently to cater
To no more Possibilities, to get
Away. Perhaps the money can be posted.
Perhaps they two may choose another Slum!
Some serious sooty half-unhappy home!—
Where loathe-love likelier may be invested.

      Keeping their scented bodies in the center
Of the hall as they walk down the hysterical hall,
They allow their lovely skirts to graze no wall,
Are off at what they manage of a canter,
And, resuming all the clues of what they were,
Try to avoid inhaling the laden air.


## FROM **CHILDREN COMING HOME**

### TINSEL MARIE

**The Coora Flower**

Today I learned the *coora* flower
grows high in the mountains of Itty-go-luba Bésa.
Province Meechee.
Pop. 39.

Now I am coming home.
This, at least, is Real, and what I know.

It was restful, learning nothing necessary.
School is tiny vacation. At least you can sleep.
At least you can think of love or feeling your boy friend against you
(which is not free from grief.)

But now it's Real Business.
I am Coming Home.

My mother will be screaming in an almost dirty dress.
The crack is gone. So a Man will be in the house.

I must watch myself.
I must not dare to sleep

### JAMAL

Nineteen Cows In A Slow Line Walking

When I was five years old
I was on a train.
From a train window I saw
nineteen cows in a slow line walking.

Each cow was behind a friend.
Except for the first cow,
who was God.

I smiled until
one cow near the end
jumped in front of a friend.

That reminded me of my mother and of my father.
It spelled what is their Together.

I was sorry for the spelling lesson.

I turned my face from the glass.

### NOVELLE

My Grandmother Is Waiting For Me To Come Home

My Grandmother is waiting for me to come home.
We live with walnuts and apples
in a one-room kitchenette above The
Some Day Liquor Gardens.

My Grandmother sits in a red rocking chair
waiting for me
to open the door with my key.

She is Black and glossy like coal.

We eat walnuts and apples,
drink root beer in cups that are broken,
above The
Some Day Liquor Gardens.

I love my Grandmother.
She is wonderful to behold
with the glossy of her coal-colored skin.
She is warm wide and long.
She laughs and she Lingers.


KOJO

**I Am A Black**

According to my Teachers,
I am now an African-American.

They call me out of my name.

BLACK is an open umbrella.
I am Black and A Black forever.

I am one of The Blacks.

We are Here, we are There.
We occur in Brazil, in Nigeria, Ghana,
in Botswana, Tanzania, in Kenya,
in Russia, Australia, in Haiti, Soweto,
in Grenada, in Cuba, in Panama, Libya,
in England and Italy, France.

We are graces in any places.
I am Black and A Black
forever.

I am other than Hyphenation.

I say, proudly, MY PEOPLE!
I say, proudly, OUR PEOPLE!

Our People do not disdain to eat yams or melons or grits
or to put peanut butter in stew.

I am Kojo. In West Afrika Kojo
means Unconquerable. My parents
named me the seventh day from my birth
in Black spirit, Black faith, Black communion.
I am Kojo. I am A Black.
And I Capitalize my name.

Do not call me out of my name.


    MERLE

Uncle Seagram

My uncle likes me too much.

I am five and a half years old, and in kindergarten.
In kindergarten everything is clean.

My uncle is six feet tall with seven bumps on his chin.
My uncle is six feet tall, and he stumbles.
He stumbles because of his Wonderful Medicine
packed in his pocket all times.

Family is ma and pa and my uncle,
three brothers, three sisters, and me.

Every night at my house we play checkers and dominoes.
My uncle sits *close*.
There aren't any shoes or socks on his feet.
Under the table a big toe tickles my ankle.
Under the oilcloth his thin knee beats into mine.
And mashes. And mashes.

When we look at TV
my uncle picks *me* to sit on his lap.
As I sit, he gets hard in the middle.
I squirm, but he keeps me, and kisses my ear.

I am not even a girl.

Once, when I went to the bathroom,
my uncle noticed, came in, shut the door,
put his long white tongue in my ear,
and whispered "We're Best Friends, and Family,
and we know how to keep Secrets."

My uncle likes me too much.
I am worried.

I do not like my uncle anymore.


## BOY BREAKING GLASS

> *To Marc Crawford*
> *from whom the commission*

Whose broken window is a cry of art
(success, that winks aware
as elegance, as a treasonable faith)
is raw: is sonic: is old-eyed première.
Our beautiful flaw and terrible ornament.
Our barbarous and metal little man.

"I shall create! If not a note, a hole.
If not an overture, a desecration."

Full of pepper and light
and Salt and night and cargoes.

"Don't go down the plank
if you see there's no extension.
Each to his grief, each to
his loneliness and fidgety revenge.
Nobody knew where I was and now I am no longer there."

The only sanity is a cup of tea.
The music is in minors.

Each one other
is having different weather.

"It was you, it was you who threw away my name!
And this is everything I have for me."

Who has not Congress, lobster, love, luau,
the Regency Room, the Statue of Liberty,
runs. A sloppy amalgamation.
A mistake.
A cliff.
A hymn, a snare, and an exceeding sun.

## MEDGAR EVERS

*For Charles Evers*

The man whose height his fear improved he
arranged to fear no further. The raw
intoxicated time was time for better birth or
a final death.

Old styles, old tempos, all the engagement of
the day—the sedate, the regulated fray—
the antique light, the Moral rose, old gusts,
tight whistlings from the past, the mothballs
in the Love at last our man forswore.

Medgar Evers annoyed confetti and assorted
brands of businessmen's eyes.

The shows came down: to maxims and surprise.
And palsy.

Roaring no rapt arise-ye to the dead, he
leaned across tomorrow. People said that
he was holding clean globes in his hands.

# THE BLACKSTONE RANGERS

I
AS SEEN BY DISCIPLINES

There they are.
Thirty at the corner.
Black, raw, ready.
Sores in the city
that do not want to heal.

II
THE LEADERS

Jeff. Gene. Geronimo. And Bop.
They cancel, cure and curry.
Hardly the dupes of the downtown thing
the cold bonbon,
the rhinestone thing. And hardly
in a hurry.
Hardly Belafonte, King,
Black Jesus, Stokely, Malcolm X or Rap.
Bungled trophies.
Their country is a Nation on no map.

Jeff, Gene, Geronimo and Bop
in the passionate noon,
in bewitching night
are the detailed men, the copious men.
They curry, cure,
they cancel, cancelled images whose Concerts
are not divine, vivacious; the different tins
are intense last entries; pagan argument;
translations of the night.

The Blackstone bitter bureaus
(bureaucracy is footloose) edit, fuse
unfashionable damnations and descent;
and exulting, monstrous hand on monstrous hand,
construct, strangely, a monstrous pearl or grace.

III
## GANG GIRLS

*A Rangerette*

Gang Girls are sweet exotics.
Mary Ann
uses the nutrients of her orient,
but sometimes sighs for Cities of blue and jewel
beyond her Ranger rim of Cottage Grove.
(Bowery Boys, Disciples, Whip-Birds will
dissolve no margins, stop no savory sanctities.)

Mary is
a rose in a whiskey glass.

Mary's
Februaries shudder and are gone. Aprils
fret frankly, lilac hurries on.
Summer is a hard irregular ridge.
October looks away.
And that's the Year!
                    Save for her bugle-love.
Save for the bleat of not-obese devotion.
Save for Somebody Terribly Dying, under
the philanthropy of robins. Save for her Ranger
bringing
an amount of rainbow in a string-drawn bag.
"Where did you get the diamond?" Do not ask:
but swallow, straight, the spirals of his flask
and assist him at your zipper; pet his lips
and help him clutch you.

Love's another departure.
Will there be any arrivals, confirmations?
Will there be gleaning?

Mary, the Shakedancer's child
from the rooming-flat, pants carefully, peers at
her laboring lover. . . .
                    Mary! Mary Ann!
Settle for sandwiches! settle for stocking caps!
for sudden blood, aborted carnival,
the props and niceties of non-loneliness—
the rhymes of Leaning.

# THE NEAR-JOHANNESBURG BOY

In South Africa the Black
children ask each other:
"Have you been detained yet?
How many times have you been
detained?"

————

The herein boy does not live
in Johannesburg. He is not
allowed to live there. Perhaps
he lives in Soweto.

My way is from woe to wonder.
A Black boy near Johannesburg, hot
in the Hot Time.

Those people
do not like Black among the colors.
They do not like our
calling our country ours.
They say our country is not ours.

Those people.
Visiting the world as I visit the world.
Those people.
Their bleach is puckered and cruel.

It is work to speak of my Father. My Father.
His body was whole till they Stopped it.
Suddenly.
With a short shot.
But, before that, physically tall and among us,
he died every day. Every moment.
My Father. . . .
First was the crumpling.
No. First was the Fist-and-the-Fury.
Last was the crumpling. It is
a little used rag that is Under, it is not,
it is not my Father gone down.

About my Mother. My Mother
was this loud laughter
below the sunshine, below the starlight at festival.
My Mother is still this loud laughter!
Still moving straight in the Getting-It-Done (as she names it).
Oh a strong eye is my Mother.
Except when it seems we are lax in our looking.

Well, enough of slump, enough of Old Story.
Like a clean spear of fire
I am moving. I am not still. I am ready
to be ready.
I shall flail
in the Hot Time.

Tonight I walk with
a hundred of playmates to where
the hurt Black of our skin is forbidden.
There, in the dark that is our dark, there,
a-pulse across earth that is our earth, there,
there exulting, there Exactly, there redeeming, there Roaring Up
(oh my Father)
we shall forge with the Fist-and-the-Fury:
we shall flail in the Hot Time:
we shall
we shall

## FROM WINNIE

II
SONG OF WINNIE

Hey Shabaka.
Donald and Dorothy and William and Mary.
Angela, Juan, Zimunya, Kimosha.
Soleiman, Onyango and Aku and Omar.
Rebecca.
Black Americans, you
wear all the names of the world!

Not a one of you ex-Afrika Blacks out there
has his or her Real Name.

I know.
You are alive. I know.
You wake, and you like the sun.
Water on your body is healing and is dear.
On your cereal the butter-rivulets
make morning art.
You prepare your hair, you
stride into the outer morning, you
are crisp and resolute and maximum.

You
don't disorder the décor
by looking at it too hard.

Well,
you don't know my people.
You don't know Keorapetse,
what he bears, has borne.

We organize our funerals.
The government has not decided
whether or not to let these latter funerals take place.
The government may decide to go ahead
                        and let those funerals proceed.
The government has not yet
made up its Mind . . .

I, Winnie, want
those funerals processed and resolved.

There is so much in my head.
Lilliesleaf; the Special Branch; and Zindzi. . . .

Childhood had a skippingtime but mostly
cow-milking, goat, and sheep, and hefty prayer,
my little sister's sickness and her death, my
mother's fierce mothering of her Given Nine,
my mother's furious faith, my mother's death,
my father's leading, modest, subtle-sassy,
my father, wise-warnful: "Get you back The Land!"

Chidhood had a skippingtime but mostly
I learned to bond the faith-steam of my mother
and the retrieval-passion of my father
and the thriving bloodfire of the Pondoland people

I try not to love me.
I try to be at big remove from me; I try
to do the good thing always because it is good.
I try not to worship my prettiest piece of pottery.
I try not to judge my berry-blue headband
a better band than Brigalia's.
The people in the roads who bow-to
are warmed by what waits in my eye for them.
The is no art, no guile, no craft, no cold breeze in my eye
to be a chopper or a going-down for them.
They say of me
"She has to fix people."
The say of me
"Hers
is a large hard beauty."

Our monsters are smashing the children.
No ribbons or shells in the chidish hair?
God must have a really fierce appetite for puzzles.

I want some settlings of these puzzles,
I want replies to whys of the human condition.

Why cannot I just go ahead and live?
Why must I keep High Arrogance at the ready?

I reverence our children.
It is bracing to be in the company of our young.
They Had the nerve to believe in common sense and goodness.

The beasts with terrible faces
are impervious to humanitarian concerns.
Humanitarianism is for other countries.

To be mechanic, automatic, Quick—
this is the way of the Time of Evil.

We have, of course and also, our Black "Statesmen."
They pour forth.
For indeed they are full.

Every day we are losing dear persons.
One of the griefs of losing,
through death, a dear person,
is that you have no longer the old delicious reasons
to say out the good Name:
"Mama!" "Sisi Vuyelwa!"
Or "George!"

I used to listen to the Elders.
"Winnie! be a nice girl!
Be a Nice Young Lady!". . . .

The difficulties of being a Nice Young Lady—
and reformer/revolutionary/pioneer!
"Strongwoman" too.

It is true I am partial to stripes.
I admire my striped scarf (and that headband.)
My Xhosa robes are sensual.
I know that I am a beautiful woman.
But Ladyhood . . . .
Ladyhood eludes me:
nor shall favor me ever.

When Botha's lieutenants
spit in my face, and pinch me,
Ladyhood eludes me.

The beasts with sick faces whom
we allowed in our land, in our living places—who
proceeded to poison our rooms—sometimes decree
there will be no singing.
(You can be shot for singing.)

Flowers, thistles, grasses,
leaves—and winds
to blow them sweetly . . . .
Oh there is so much calling and murmuring and pulsing and beating
       about in my head.
In dreams
I *think* I'm always firmly what I know myself to be.

White pelicans in Uganda,
dipping beautifully
and in unison to
achieve their fish . . . .

There is, still, loveliness in the world:
in Uganda: in Kenya:
even here—
this home
heart-halting, perverse.

There are millions of words in this world.
Not necessarily may be found, all cooked,
the ones to express *my* nuances.

Yet I know
that I am Poet!
I pass you my Poem.

A poem doesn't do everything for you.
You are supposed to go *on* with your thinking.
You are supposed to enrich
the other person's poem with your extensions,
your uniquely personal understandings,
thus making the poem serve *you.*

I pass you my Poem!—to tell you
we are all vulnerable—
the midget, the Mighty,
the richest, the poor.
Men, women, children, and trees.
I am vulnerable.
Hector Petersen was vulnerable.

My Poem is life, and not finished.
It shall never be finished.
My Poem is life, and can grow.

Wherever life can grow, it will.
It will sprout out,
and do the best it can.
I give you what I have.
You don't get all your questions answered in this world.
How many answers shall be found
in the developing world of my Poem?
I don't know. Nevertheless I put my Poem,
which is my life, into your hands, where it will
do the best it can.

I am not a tight-faced Poet.

I am tired of little tight-faced poets sitting down to
shape perfect unimportant pieces.
Poems that cough lightly—catch back a sneeze.
This is the time for Big Poems,
roaring up out of sleaze,
poems from ice, from vomit, and from tainted blood.
This is the time for stiff *or* viscous poems.
Big, and Big . . .

## TO AN OLD BLACK WOMAN, HOMELESS AND INDISTINCT

I.

Your every day is a pilgrimage.
A blue hubbub.
Your days are collected bacchanals of fear and self-troubling.

And your nights! Your nights.
When you put you down in alley or cardboard or viaduct,
your lovers are rats, finding your secret places.

II.

When you rise in another morning,
you hit the street, your incessant enemy.

See? Here you are, in the so-busy world.
You walk. You walk.
You pass The People.
No. The People pass you.

Here's a Rich Girl marching briskly to her charms.
She is suede and scarf and belting and perfume.
She sees you not, she sees you very well.
At five in the afternoon Miss Rich Girl will go Home
to brooms and vacuum cleaner and carpeting,
two cats, two marble-top tables, two telephones,
shiny green peppers, flowers in impudent vases,
visitors.
Before all that there's luncheon to be known.
Lasagna, lobster salad, sandwiches.
All day there's coffee to be loved.
There are luxuries
of minor dissatisfaction, luxuries of Plan.

III.

That's *her* story.
*You're* going to vanish, not necessarily nicely, fairly soon.
Although essentially dignity itself a death
is not necessarily tidy, modest or discreet.
When they find you
your legs may not be tidy nor aligned.
Your mouth may be all crooked or destroyed.

Black old woman, homeless, indistinct—
Your last and least adventure is Review.
    Folks used to celebrate your birthday!
Folks used to say "She's such a pretty little thing!"
Folks used to say "She draws such handsome horses, cows and
    houses."
Folks used to say "That child is going far."

# GLORIA ODEN

## (B. 1923)

*Unjustly underknown, the poems of Gloria Oden are, at their best, acutely chiseled lyrics full of humor and sadness in the twentieth-century tradition of Marianne Moore, Louise Bogan, and Elizabeth Bishop. Ms. Oden's subject matter is often somehow linked with loss—of innocence, a friend who has moved, a love—but she deals with the experience at a remove that precludes pathos. Gloria Oden grew up as a minister's daughter in Yonkers, New York, during the Depression. She is professor of English at the University of Maryland, Baltimore County, and has been honored by the John Hay Whitney Foundation, Yaddo, and the National Endowment for the Humanities.*

## A PRIVATE LETTER TO BRAZIL

The map shows me where it is you are. I
am here, where the words NEW YORK run an inch
out to sea, ending where GULF STREAM flows by.

The coastline bristles with place names. The pinch
in printing space has launched them offshore
with the fish-bone's fine-tooth spread, to clinch

their urban identity. Much more
noticeable it is in the chain
of hopscotching islands that, loosely, moors

your continent to mine. (Already plain
is its eastward drift, and who could say
what would become of it left free!) Again,

the needle-pine alignment round S/A,
while where it is you are (or often go),
RIO, spills its subtle phonic bouquet

farthest seawards of all. Out there I know
the sounding is some deep 2000 feet,
and the nationalized current tours so

pregnant with resacas. In their flux meets
all the subtlety of God's great nature
and man's terse grief. See, Hero, at your feet

is not that slight tossing dead Leander?


## TESTAMENT OF LOSS

You would think that night could lift;
that something of light would sift
through to gray its thick self
sealing.

It's five years, now.
Still black gloams over
day unable to slip
across my sill
one finger
to raise its white form
of hope.


## BIBLE STUDY

In the old testament
"Hizzoner" was forever
singling out someone
to speak with.
Dream
and he would make
a visit.
Cruise the world
from your favorite
mountain top
and he would come
to call.

Even out of the garrulous
mouth of the whirlwind
he would fetch
himself forth
for a bit of
spirited conversation.
Indeed,
he was apt to
catch up with you
at the most staggering
of times,
and in the most debatable
of places.

So, I think,
he does still.
Who else, my dear
could have snapped us
together and put us
so warmly to bed?

What puzzles me now
is our particular whirlwind.
Tell me,
did the Old Guy
trumpet us out of
your upset
or mine?

# MARI EVANS

## (B. 1923)

*Mari Evans was born in Toledo, Ohio. Her deceptively simple poems
often feature the rich use of everyday speech to surprising poetic ef-
fect. Gifted and experienced in many areas, she has taught at Indiana,
Northwestern, and Washington universities, the State University of
New York at Albany, and Cornell, and has worked in television, in-*

cluding producing and directing her own weekly television show, "The Black Experience." Her work as a poet has received worldwide recognition in anthologies and prizes, and she has also written journalism, children's books, and music. In 1965, Mari Evans was named a John Hay Whitney Fellow, and in 1970 she was the second recipient of the Black Academy of Arts and Letters Poetry Prize.


## WHEN IN ROME

Mattie dear
the box is full
take
whatever you like
to eat
       (an egg
       or soup
       . . . there ain't no meat)
there's endive there
and
cottage cheese
       (whew! if I had some
       black-eyed peas . . . )
there's sardines
on the shelves
and such
but
don't
get my anchovies

they cost
too much!
       (me get the
       anchovies indeed!
       what she think, she got—
       a bird to feed?)
there's plenty in there
to fill you up.
       (yes'm. just the
       sight's
       enough!

Hope I lives till I get
home
I'm tired of eatin'
what they eats in Rome . . . )

# DOLORES KENDRICK

## (B. 1927)

*"You smile on your disasters. Can it be that you,/someday, will illuminate the darkness of this song!" That is one of the epigraphs in Dolores Kendrick's third book of poems, and it aptly describes her work as she considers, imagines, and speaks for black women in the nineteenth century with grace, compassion, and humor. Ms. Kendrick's ability to be accurate without sentimentality and her willingness to embrace all areas of these women's lives, good as well as bad, allow her to do them justice, and they exist on the page as fully realized persons. Dolores Kendrick is a native of Washington, D.C., where she still resides when not teaching English at Phillips Exeter in New Hampshire.*

## JENNY IN LOVE

Danced in the evenin'

          while

the supper
burn;

whupped

          in the morning:

danced again!

## SOPHIE, CLIMBING THE STAIRS

*One* / O-N-E

*Stair* / S-T-A-I-R

*Two* / T-W-O

*Stairs* / S-T-A-I-R-S

(gotta remember the *S*, mo' than one!)

This learnin' to count and spell at the same time
be a nuisance, but I've gotta do it. Only way

to learn somethin' in this world. Thank the lawd for
Uncle James. He knows how to read and write and count!

Massa's got nothin' on him!

*Five* / F-I-V-E

*Stairs* / S-T-A-I-R-S

Run outta stairs soon, then where will you be, Sophie?
Run outta breath, too, then what use are you, Sophie?
But these stairs be of no use, no use at all, unless
they hep Sophie walk her way up to readin' and writin'.

Uncle James' idea. Good one, too.

*Eight* / E-I-G-H-T

Strange sound; *eight* with an E. Why don't they spell *ate*
with an *E*, too, sound the same, don't make sense. Should be
an *A*, but no I heard Massa spell somethin' out to Missus

the other day ('cause he didn't want me to know what he was sayin')
and he mentioned *eight* and spelled it with an *E*. I remembered
the letters and told Uncle James and he told me *eight*, come to

think of it, I remembered all the letters Massa spelled out
and Uncle James told me everything he said. Poor Ole Massa
had lost eight dollars that day gamblin' on a dog fight.

He needed to borrow ten more dollars from Missus to pay his debts
around the town. Well, he got me free, almost, paid about twelve
hundred dollars for me, but I worked that off long ago.

Right now, I'm profit.

*Twelve* / T-W-E-L-V-E

Finished. At the top. Days gettin' longer and my breath
gettin' shorter, but my memory be still young and askin'.
There be the period and the commas, the stops and the shorts,
And the periods put an end to everything and don't let you go
no further, don't play 'round with periods, Uncle James says,
they the be-all and end-all, don't believe in takin' long walks

in the fields when you're tired, don't believe in too much moanin'
and misery, just bring things into focus when you least 'spect
and bring the Lawd's truth up to your doorsill, if you can.

No, don't fool 'round with them periods. Got lots of them in my
pocket. Savin' them for my children when they ole enough to spend
    them.

But the comma, gotta learn that better. Say my prayers with a period.
Listen to Missus with a comma.

*Twelve tribes of Israel*
*sittin' in a tree,*

*Daniel in the Lion's mouth,*
*Lawd, deliver me!*

Take this hot milk to Missus' room and see if the two of them
start spellin' things out again that they don't want me to know.

Wants to know the baptism of words.

## JENNY IN SLEEP

Nothin' be as terrible

> as sleep

nothin'
be as bright, either.

I come and go

> as I please.


## SADIE SNUFFS A CANDLE

It be the last time I'm snuffin' candles in cold dark
    halls, nobody there but me
        waitin' to be called on
           and do errands.

Now, I'm twenty.
Tomorrow I go to my freedom.

My mistress and me go together.
She leaves a terrible house.
I leaves a dead one.

Her husband decayin' while he still alive,
dyin' in her body while he heats and sweats.

My husband a thief, jackassin' 'round, 'till he be shot
    with a chicken under his coat.

Nonny and me.
We escape together, the two of us:

She say she a slave, too,
not all slaves black and poor,
and she wants her freedom.

I gives it to her
with my spirit movin'
in her shoes.

She gives it back, though
between us it be
a little tattered.

Nonny and me: we each other's age. I her servant,
    she, mine. Good person.

Tonight be the final one.
She sit at the head of the table
for the last time.

Then.

I snuff out with my fingertips
the big lonesome candle
in the wide, broodin' hall.

We now be shadows
still and apart
me and the candle.

I leaves first, then missus leave behind me.
    We travel
            *Goodbye, dear Sadie!*
                    different ways.

I smell the candle's taper
from the open doorway,
smoke shadows in a rich, black light:

the end of the burnin'.

                *Hey, Nonny! Go!*

# RAYMOND PATTERSON

## (B. 1929)

*Raymond Patterson was born in Harlem and grew up in the New York metropolitan area. Educated at Lincoln University and New York University, in 1969 he published* Twenty-Six Ways of Looking at a Black Man, *the title poem of which is an astonishing achievement. Bowing to Wallace Stevens, the poem moves through a series of vignettes and postulations variously humorous and philosophical, visual and blues-tinged. Mr. Patterson has, throughout his career, remained close to the blues, and has published a volume of poems in blues stanzas. Mr. Patterson has taught for many years at the City University of New York and lives with his family on Long Island.*

## TWENTY-SIX WAYS OF LOOKING AT A BLACKMAN

*For Boydie & Ama*

### I

On the road we met a blackman,
But no one else.

### II

Dreams are reunions. Who has not
On occasion entertained the presence
Of a blackman?

### III

From brown paper bags
A blackman fills the vacancies of morning
With orange speculations.

IV

Always I hope to find
The blackman I know,
Or one who knows him.

V

Devouring earthly possessions
Is one of a blackman's excesses.
Exaggerating their transiency
Is another.

VI

Even this shadow has weight.
A cool heaviness.
Call it a blackman's ghost.

VII

The possibilities of color
Were choices made by the eye
Looking inward.
The possibilities of rhythms
For a blackman are predetermined.

VIII

When it had all been unravelled,
The blackman found that it had been
Entirely woven of black thread.

IX

Children who loved him
Hid him from the world
By pretending he was a blackman.

X

The fingerprints of a blackman
Were on her pillow. Or was it
Her luminous tears?
. . . An absence, or a presence?
Only when it was darker
Would she know.

### XI

The blackman dipped water
From a well.
And when the well dried,
He dipped cool blackness.

### XII

We are told that the seeds
Of rainbows are not unlike
A blackman's tear.

### XIII

What is more beautiful than black flowers,
Or blackmen in fields
Gathering them?
. . . The bride, or the wedding?

### XIV

When it was finished,
Some of the carvers of Destiny
Would sigh in relief,
But the blackman would sigh in intaglio,
Having shed vain illusions in mastering the stone.

### XV

Affirmation of negatives:
A blackman trembles
That his thoughts run toward darkness.

### XVI

The odor of a blackman derives
No less from the sweat of his apotheosis,
Than emanation of crushed apples
He carries in his arms.

### XVII

If I could imagine the shaping of Fate,
I would think of blackmen
Handling the sun.

### XVIII

Is it harvest time in the brown fields,
Or is it just a black man
Singing?

### XIX

There is the sorrow of blackmen
Lost in cities. But who can conceive
Of cities lost in a blackman?

### XX

A small boy lifts a seashell
To his listening ear.
It is the blackman again,
Whispering his sagas of drowned sailors.

### XXI

At the cradle of Justice were found
Three gifts: a pair of scales, a sword,
And a simple cloth. But the Magi had departed.
Several who were with us agreed
One of the givers must have been
A blackman.

### XXII

As vines grow towards light,
So roots grow towards darkness.
Back and forth a blackman goes,
Gathering the harvest.

### XXIII

By moonlight
We tossed our pebbles into the lake
And marveled
At the beauty of concentric sorrows.
You thought it was like the troubled heart
Of a blackman,
Because of the dancing light.

XXIV

As the time of our leave taking drew near,
The blackman blessed each of us
By pronouncing the names of his children.

XXV

As I remember it,
The only unicorn in the park
Belonged to a blackman
Who went about collecting bits
And torn scraps of afternoons.

XXVI

At the center of Being
Said the blackman,
All is tangential.
Even this laughter, even your tears.

■

# DEREK WALCOTT

(B. 1930)

*In his early poem "A Far Cry from Africa," Derek Walcott wrestles with the dilemma of those of African descent in the New World: "I who am poisoned with the blood of both, / Where shall I turn, divided to the vein?" In a later poem, "The Schooner* Flight," *Walcott proposes an answer: "I have Dutch, nigger, and English in me, / and either I'm nobody, or I'm a nation." Walcott has made the most of these tensions, constructing a body of work that stands firmly in the highest tradition of the English language while remaining true to his birth and upbringing as a person of color in the Caribbean, weaving a literature of the archipelagoes in the cadences of Shakespeare, Auden, and the King James Bible. In fact, it can be said that Walcott, in works like "The Sea Is History" and* Omeros, *is creating a myth of the Caribbean, full of history and bright, clear vistas of water and sky. Derek Walcott began as an artist at a young age, publishing a poem at fourteen, and studying painting (he is also an extraordinary visual artist).*

*He was educated at the University of the West Indies in Jamaica, and has worked as a reviewer, critic, and theater director. Since the early seventies, Mr. Walcott has spent much of his time in the United States, teaching at Harvard and Boston universities. His work has been richly honored, with a MacArthur Fellowship, the Queen's Medal for Poetry, and, in 1992, the Nobel Prize for Literature. In praise, the Nobel committee said, "In his literary works Walcott has laid a course for his own cultural environment, but through them he speaks to each and every one of us. In him, the West Indian culture has found its great poet."*

## A FAR CRY FROM AFRICA

A wind is ruffling the tawny pelt
Of Africa. Kikuyu, quick as flies,
Batten upon the bloodstreams of the veldt.
Corpses are scattered through a paradise.
Only the worm, colonel of carrion, cries:
"Waste no compassion on these separate dead!"
Statistics justify and scholars seize
The salients of colonial policy.
What is that to the white child hacked in bed?
To savages, expendable as Jews?

Threshed out by beaters, the long rushes break
In a white dust of ibises whose cries
Have wheeled since civilization's dawn
From the parched river or beast-teeming plain.
The violence of beast on beast is read
As natural law, but upright man
Seeks his divinity by inflicting pain.
Delirious as these worried beasts, his wars
Dance to the tightened carcass of a drum,
While he calls courage still that native dread
Of the white peace contracted by the dead.

Again brutish necessity wipes its hands
Upon the napkin of a dirty cause, again
A waste of our compassion, as with Spain,
The gorilla wrestles with the superman.

I who am poisoned with the blood of both,
Where shall I turn, divided to the vein?
I who have cursed
The drunken officer of British rule, how choose
Between this Africa and the English tongue I love?
Betray them both, or give back what they give?
How can I face such slaughter and be cool?
How can I turn from Africa and live?

## THE FIST

The fist clenched round my heart
loosens a little, and I gasp
brightness; but it tightens
again. When have I ever not loved
the pain of love? But this has moved

past love to mania. This has the strong
clench of the madman, this is
gripping the ledge of unreason, before
plunging howling into the abyss.

Hold hard then, heart. This way at least you live.

## THE SCHOONER *FLIGHT*

1   *Adios, Carenage*

In idle August, while the sea soft,
and leaves of brown islands stick to the rim
of this Caribbean, I blow out the light
by the dreamless face of Maria Concepcion
to ship as a seaman on the schooner *Flight*.
Out in the yard turning grey in the dawn,
I stood like a stone and nothing else move
but the cold sea rippling like galvanize
and the nail holes of stars in the sky roof,
till a wind start to interfere with the trees.

I pass me dry neighbour sweeping she yard
as I went downhill, and I nearly said:
"Sweep soft, you witch, 'cause she don't sleep hard,"
but the bitch look through me like I was dead.
A route taxi pull up, park-lights still on.
The driver size up my bags with a grin:
"This time, Shabine, like you really gone!"
I ain't answer the ass, I simply pile in
the back seat and watch the sky burn
above Laventille pink as the gown
in which the woman I left was sleeping,
and I look in the rearview and see a man
exactly like me, and the man was weeping
for the houses, the streets, that whole fucking island.
Christ have mercy on all sleeping things!
From that dog rotting down Wrightson Road
to when I was a dog on these streets;
if loving these islands must be my load,
out of corruption my soul takes wings.
But they had started to poison my soul
with their big house, big car, big-time bohbohl,
coolie, nigger, Syrian, and French Creole,
so I leave it for them and their carnival—
I taking a sea-bath, I gone down the road.
I know these islands from Monos to Nassau,
a rusty head sailor with sea-green eyes
that they nickname Shabine, the patois for
any red nigger, and I, Shabine, saw
when these slums of empire was paradise.
I'm just a red nigger who love the sea,
I had a sound colonial education,
I have Dutch, nigger, and English in me,
and either I'm nobody, or I'm a nation.

But Maria Concepcion was all my thought
watching the sea heaving up and down
as the port side of dories, schooners, and yachts
was painted afresh by the strokes of the sun
signing her name with every reflection;
I knew when dark-haired evening put on
her bright silk at sunset, and, folding the sea,
sidled under the sheet with her starry laugh,
that there'd be no rest, there'd be no forgetting.

Is like telling mourners round the graveside
about resurrection, they want the dead back,
so I smile to myself as the bow rope untied
and the *Flight* swing seaward: "Is no use repeating
that the sea have more fish. I ain't want her
dressed in the sexless light of a seraph,
I want those round brown eyes like a marmoset, and
till the day when I can lean back and laugh,
those claws that tickled my back on sweating
Sunday afternoons, like a crab on wet sand."
As I worked, watching the rotting waves come
past the bow that scissor the sea like silk,
I swear to you all, by my mother's milk,
by the stars that shall fly from tonight's furnace,
that I loved them, my children, my wife, my home;
I loved them as poets love the poetry
that kills them, as drowned sailors the sea.

You ever look up from some lonely beach
and see a far schooner? Well, when I write
this poem, each phrase go be soaked in salt;
I go draw and knot every line as tight
as ropes in this rigging; in simple speech
my common language go be the wind,
my pages the sails of the schooner *Flight*.
But let me tell you how this business begin.


2   *Raptures of the Deep*

Smuggled Scotch for O'Hara, big government man,
between Cedros and the Main, so the Coast Guard couldn't
     touch us,
and the Spanish pirogues always met us halfway,
but a voice kept saying: "Shabine, see this business
of playing pirate?" Well, so said, so done!
That whole racket crash. And I for a woman,
for her laces and silks, Maria Concepcion.
Ay, ay! Next thing I hear, some Commission of Enquiry
was being organized to conduct a big quiz,
with himself as chairman investigating himself.
Well, I knew damn well who the suckers would be,
not that shark in shark skin, but his pilot fish,
khaki-pants red niggers like you and me.

What worse, I fighting with Maria Concepcion,
plates flying and thing, so I swear: "Not again!"
It was mashing up my house and my family.
I was so broke all I needed was shades and a cup
or four shades and four cups in four-cup Port of Spain;
all the silver I had was the coins on the sea.

You saw them ministers in *The Express*,
guardians of the poor—one hand at their back,
and one set o' police only guarding their house,
and the Scotch pouring in through the back door.
As for that minister-monster who smuggled the booze,
that half-Syrian saurian, I got so vex to see
that face thick with powder, the warts, the stone lids
like a dinosaur caked with primordial ooze
by the lightning of flashbulbs sinking in wealth,
that I said: "Shabine, this is shit, understand!"
But he get somebody to kick my crutch out his office
like I was some artist! That bitch was so grand,
couldn't get off his high horse and kick me himself.
I have seen things that would make a slave sick
in this Trinidad, the Limers' Republic.

I couldn't shake the sea noise out of my head,
the shell of my ears sang Maria Concepcion,
so I start salvage diving with a crazy Mick,
name O'Shaughnessy, and a limey named Head;
but this Caribbean so choke with the dead
that when I would melt in emerald water,
whose ceiling rippled like a silk tent,
I saw them corals: brain, fire, sea-fans,
dead-men's-fingers, and then, the dead men.
I saw that the powdery sand was their bones
ground white from Senegal to San Salvador,
so, I panic third dive, and surface for a month
in the Seamen's Hostel. Fish broth and sermons.
When I thought of the woe I had brought my wife,
when I saw my worries with that other woman,
I wept under water, salt seeking salt,
for her beauty had fallen on me like a sword
cleaving me from my children, flesh of my flesh!

There was this barge from St. Vincent, but she was too deep
to float her again. When we drank, the limey
got tired of my sobbing for Maria Concepcion.
He said he was getting the bends. Good for him!
The pain in my heart for Maria Concepcion,
the hurt I had done to my wife and children,
was worse than the bends. In the rapturous deep
there was no cleft rock where my soul could hide
like the boobies each sunset, no sandbar of light
where I could rest, like the pelicans know,
so I got raptures once, and I saw God
like a harpooned grouper bleeding, and a far
voice was rumbling, "Shabine, if you leave her,
if you leave her, I shall give you the morning star."
When I left the madhouse I tried other women
but, once they stripped naked, their spiky cunts
bristled like sea-eggs and I couldn't dive.
The chaplain came round. I paid him no mind.
Where is my rest place, Jesus? Where is my harbour?
Where is the pillow I will not have to pay for,
and the window I can look from that frames my life?

### 3   Shabine Leaves the Republic

I had no nation now but the imagination.
After the white man, the niggers didn't want me
when the power swing to their side.
The first chain my hands and apologize, "History";
the next said I wasn't black enough for their pride.
Tell me, what power, on these unknown rocks—
a spray-plane Air Force, the Fire Brigade,
the Red Cross, the Regiment, two, three police dogs
that pass before you finish bawling "Parade!"?
I met History once, but he ain't recognize me,
a parchment Creole, with warts
like an old sea-bottle, crawling like a crab
through the holes of shadow cast by the net
of a grille balcony; cream linen, cream hat.
I confront him and shout, "Sir, is Shabine!
They say I'se your grandson. You remember Grandma,
your black cook, at all?" The bitch hawk and spat.
A spit like that worth any number of words.
But that's all them bastards have left us: words.

I no longer believed in the revolution.
I was losing faith in the love of my woman.
I had seen that moment Aleksandr Blok
crystallize in *The Twelve*. Was between
the Police Marine Branch and Hotel Venezuelana
one Sunday at noon. Young men without flags
using shirts, their chests waiting for holes.
They kept marching into the mountains, and
their noise ceased as foam sinks into sand.
They sank in the bright hills like rain, every one
with his own nimbus, leaving shirts in the street,
and the echo of power at the end of the street.
Propeller-blade fans turn over the Senate;
the judges, they say, still sweat in carmine,
on Frederick Street the idlers all marching
by standing still, the Budget turns a new leaf.
In the 12:30 movies the projectors best
not break down, or you go see revolution. Aleksandr Blok
enters and sits in the third row of pit eating choc-
olate cone, waiting for a spaghetti West-
ern with Clint Eastwood and featuring Lee Van Cleef.


4   *The* Flight, *Passing Blanchisseuse*

Dusk. The *Flight* passing Blanchisseuse.
Gulls wheel like from a gun again,
and foam gone amber that was white,
lighthouse and star start making friends,
down every beach the long day ends,
and there, on that last stretch of sand,
on a beach bare of all but light,
dark hands start pulling in the seine
of the dark sea, deep, deep inland.


5   *Shabine Encounters the Middle Passage*

Man, I brisk in the galley first thing next dawn,
brewing li'l coffee; fog coil from the sea
like the kettle steaming when I put it down
slow, slow, 'cause I couldn't believe what I see:
where the horizon was one silver haze,
the fog swirl and swell into sails, so close
that I saw it was sails, my hair grip my skull,

it was horrors, but it was beautiful.
We float through a rustling forest of ships
with sails dry like paper, behind the glass
I saw men with rusty eyeholes like cannons,
and whenever their half-naked crews cross the sun,
right through their tissue, you traced their bones
like leaves against the sunlight; frigates, barkentines,
the backward-moving current swept them on,
and high on their decks I saw great admirals,
Rodney, Nelson, de Grasse, I heard the hoarse orders
they gave those Shabines, and the forest
of masts sail right through the *Flight*,
and all you could hear was the ghostly sound
of waves rustling like grass in a low wind
and the hissing weeds they trailed from the stern;
slowly they heaved past from east to west
like this round world was some cranked water wheel,
every ship pouring like a wooden bucket
dredged from the deep; my memory revolve
on all sailors before me, then the sun
heat the horizon's ring and they was mist.

Next we pass slave ships. Flags of all nations,
our fathers below deck too deep, I suppose,
to hear us shouting. So we stop shouting. Who knows
who his grandfather is, much less his name?
Tomorrow our landfall will be the Barbados.

6    *The Sailor Sings Back to the Casuarinas*

You see them on the low hills of Barbados
bracing like windbreaks, needles for hurricanes,
trailing, like masts, the cirrus of torn sails;
when I was green like them, I used to think
those cypresses, leaning against the sea,
that take the sea-noise up into their branches,
are not real cypresses but casuarinas.
Now captain just call them Canadian cedars.
But cedars, cypresses, or casuarinas,
whoever called them so had a good cause,
watching their bending bodies wail like women
after a storm, when some schooner came home
with news of one more sailor drowned again.

Once the sound "cypress" used to make more sense
than the green "casuarinas," though, to the wind
whatever grief bent them was all the same,
since they were trees with nothing else in mind
but heavenly leaping or to guard a grave;
but we live like our names and you would have
to be colonial to know the difference,
to know the pain of history words contain,
to love those trees with an inferior love,
and to believe: "Those casuarinas bend
like cypresses, their hair hangs down in rain
like sailors' wives. They're classic trees, and we,
if we live like the names our masters please,
by careful mimicry might become men."

7    *The* Flight *Anchors in Castries Harbor*

When the stars self were young over Castries,
I loved you alone and I loved the whole world.
What does it matter that our lives are different?
Burdened with the loves of our different children?
When I think of your young face washed by the wind
and your voice that chuckles in the slap of the sea?
The lights are out on La Toc promontory,
except for the hospital. Across at Vigie
the marina arcs keep vigil. I have kept my own
promise, to leave you the one thing I own,
you whom I loved first: my poetry.
We here for one night. Tomorrow, the *Flight* will be gone.

8    *Fight with the Crew*

It had one bitch on board, like he had me mark—
that was the cook, some Vincentian arse
with a skin like a gommier tree, red peeling bark,
and wash-out blue eyes; he wouldn't give me a ease,
like he feel he was white. Had an exercise book,
this same one here, that I was using to write
my poetry, so one day this man snatch it
from my hand, and start throwing it left and right

to the rest of the crew, bawling out, "Catch it,"
and start mincing me like I was some hen
because of the poems. Some case is for fist,
some case is for tholing pin, some is for knife—
this one was for knife. Well, I beg him first,
but he keep reading, "O my children, my wife,"
and playing he crying, to make the crew laugh;
it move like a flying fish, the silver knife
that catch him right in the plump of his calf,
and he faint so slowly, and he turn more white
than he thought he was. I suppose among men
you need that sort of thing. It ain't right
but that's how it is. There wasn't much pain,
just plenty blood, and Vincie and me best friend,
but none of them go fuck with my poetry again.

### 9 *Maria Concepcion & the Book of Dreams*

The jet that was screeching over the *Flight*
was opening a curtain into the past.
"Dominica ahead!"
                                    "It still have Caribs there."
"One day go be planes only, no more boat."
"Vince, God ain't make nigger to fly through the air."
"Progress, Shabine, that's what it's all about.
Progress leaving all we small islands behind."
I was at the wheel, Vince sitting next to me
gaffing. Crisp, bracing day. A high-running sea.
"Progress is something to ask Caribs about.
They kill them by millions, some in war,
some by forced labour dying in the mines
looking for silver, after that niggers; more
progress. Until I see definite signs
that mankind change, Vince, I ain't want to hear.
Progress is history's dirty joke.
Ask that sad green island getting nearer."
Green islands, like mangoes pickled in brine.
In such fierce salt let my wound be healed,
me, in my freshness as a seafarer.

That night, with the sky sparks frosty with fire,
I ran like a Carib through Dominica,
my nose holes choked with memory of smoke;
I heard the screams of my burning children,
I ate the brains of mushrooms, the fungi
of devil's parasols under white, leprous rocks;
my breakfast was leaf mould in leaking forests,
with leaves big as maps, and when I heard noise
of the soldiers' progress through the thick leaves,
though my heart was bursting, I get up and ran
through the blades of balisier sharper than spears;
with the blood of my race, I ran, boy, I ran
with moss-footed speed like a painted bird;
then I fall, but I fall by an icy stream under
cool fountains of fern, and a screaming parrot
catch the dry branches and I drowned at last
in big breakers of smoke; then when that ocean
of black smoke pass, and the sky turn white,
there was nothing but Progress, if Progress is
an iguana as still as a young leaf in sunlight.
I bawl for Maria, and her *Book of Dreams*.

It anchored her sleep, that insomniac's Bible,
a soiled orange booklet with a cyclops' eye
center, from the Dominican Republic.
Its coarse pages were black with the usual
symbols of prophecy, in excited Spanish;
an open palm upright, sectioned and numbered
like a butcher chart, delivered the future.
One night, in a fever, radiantly ill,
she say, "Bring me the book, the end has come."
She said: "I dreamt of whales and a storm,"
but for that dream, the book had no answer.
A next night I dreamed of three old women
featureless as silkworms, stitching my fate,
and I scream at them to come out my house,
and I try beating them away with a broom,
but as they go out, so they crawl back again,
until I start screaming and crying, my flesh
raining with sweat, and she ravage the book
for the dream meaning, and there was nothing;
my nerves melt like a jellyfish—that was when I broke—
they found me round the Savannah, screaming:

All you see me talking to the wind, so you think I mad.
Well, Shabine has bridled the horses of the sea;
you see me watching the sun till my eyeballs seared,
so all you mad people feel Shabine crazy,
but all you ain't know my strength, hear? The coconuts
standing by in their regiments in yellow khaki,
they waiting for Shabine to take over these islands,
and all you best dread the day I am healed
of being a human. All you fate in my hand,
ministers, businessmen, Shabine have you, friend,
I shall scatter your lives like a handful of sand,
I who have no weapon but poetry and
the lances of palms and the sea's shining shield!

### 10  *Out of the Depths*

Next day, dark sea. A arse-aching dawn.
"Damn wind shift sudden as a woman mind."
The slow swell start cresting like some mountain range
with snow on the top.
           "Ay, Skipper, sky dark!"
"This ain't right for August."
           "This light damn strange,
this season, sky should be clear as a field."

A stingray steeplechase across the sea,
tail whipping water, the high man-o'-wars
start reeling inland, quick, quick an archery
of flying fish miss us! Vince say: "You notice?"
and a black-mane squall pounce on the sail
like a dog on a pigeon, and it snap the neck
of the *Flight* and shake it from head to tail.
"Be Jesus, I never see sea get so rough
so fast! That wind come from God back pocket!"
"Where Cap'n headin? Like the man gone blind!"
"If we's to drong, we go drong, Vince, fock-it!"
"Shabine, say your prayers, if life leave you any!"

I have not loved those that I loved enough.
Worse than the mule kick of Kick-'Em-Jenny
Channel, rain start to pelt the *Flight* between
mountains of water. If I was frighten?

The tent poles of water spouts bracing the sky
start wobbling, clouds unstitch at the seams
and sky water drench us, and I hear myself cry,
"I'm the drowned sailor in her *Book of Dreams*."
I remembered them ghost ships, I saw me corkscrewing
to the sea-bed of sea-worms, fathom pass fathom,
my jaw clench like a fist, and only one thing
hold me, trembling, how my family safe home.
Then a strength like it seize me and the strength said:
"I from backward people who still fear God."
Let Him, in His might, heave Leviathan upward
by the winch of His will, the beast pouring lace
from his sea-bottom bed; and that was the faith
that had fade from a child in the Methodist chapel
in Chisel Street, Castries, when the whale-bell
sang service and, in hard pews ribbed like the whale,
proud with despair, we sang how our race
survive the sea's maw, our history, our peril,
and now I was ready for whatever death will.
But if that storm had strength, was in Cap'n face,
beard beading with spray, tears salting the eyes,
crucify to his post, that nigger hold fast
to that wheel, man, like the cross held Jesus,
and the wounds of his eyes like they crying for us,
and I feeding him white rum, while every crest
with Leviathan-lash make the *Flight* quail
like two criminal. Whole night, with no rest,
till red-eyed like dawn, we watch our travail
subsiding, subside, and there was no more storm.
And the noon sea get calm as Thy Kingdom come.


    11   *After the Storm*

There's a fresh light that follows a storm
while the whole sea still havoc; in its bright wake
I saw the veiled face of Maria Concepcion
marrying the ocean, then drifting away
in the widening lace of her bridal train
with white gulls her bridesmaids, till she was gone.
I wanted nothing after that day.
Across my own face, like the face of the sun,
a light rain was falling, with the sea calm.

Fall gently, rain, on the sea's upturned face
like a girl showering; make these islands fresh
as Shabine once knew them! Let every trace,
every hot road, smell like clothes she just press
and sprinkle with drizzle. I finish dream;
whatever the rain wash and the sun iron:
the white clouds, the sea and sky with one seam,
is clothes enough for my nakedness.
Though my *Flight* never pass the incoming tide
of this inland sea beyond the loud reefs
of the final Bahamas, I am satisfied
if my hand gave voice to one people's grief.
Open the map. More islands there, man,
than peas on a tin plate, all different size,
one thousand in the Bahamas alone,
from mountains to low scrub with coral keys,
and from this bowsprit, I bless every town,
the blue smell of smoke in hills behind them,
and the one small road winding down them like twine
to the roofs below; I have only one theme:
The bowsprit, the arrow, the longing, the lunging heart—
the flight to a target whose aim we'll never know,
vain search for one island that heals with its harbour
and a guiltless horizon, where the almond's shadow
doesn't injure the sand. There are so many islands!
As many islands as the stars at night
on that branched tree from which meteors are shaken
like falling fruit around the schooner *Flight*.
But things must fall, and so it always was,
on one hand Venus, on the other Mars;
fall, and are one, just as this earth is one
island in archipelagoes of stars.
My first friend was the sea. Now, is my last.
I stop talking now. I work, then I read,
cotching under a lantern hooked to the mast.
I try to forget what happiness was,
and when that don't work, I study the stars.
Sometimes is just me, and the soft-scissored foam
as the deck turn white and the moon open
a cloud like a door, and the light over me
is a road in white moonlight taking me home.
Shabine sang to you from the depths of the sea.

# EULOGY TO W. H. AUDEN

*(Read at the Cathedral of St. John the Divine,
New York, October 17, 1983)*

I

Assuredly, that fissured face
is wincing deeply, and must loathe
our solemn rubbish,
frown on our canonizing farce
as self-enhancing, in lines both
devout and snobbish.

Yet it may spare us who convene
against its wish in varnished pews
this autumn evening;
as maps remember countries, mien
defines a man, and his appears
at our beseeching.

Each granite feature, cracked and plain
as the ground in Giotto, is
apt to this chancel,
the wry mouth bracketed with pain,
the lizard eyes whose motto is:
Opposites cancel.

For further voices will delight
in all that left the body of
the mortal Auden
centuries after candlelit
Kirchstetten freed its tenant of
Time and its burden;

for what we cherish is as much
our own fate, stricken with the light
of his strange calling,
and, once we leave this darkened church
and stand on pavements in the night
to see a falling

leaf like a seraph sign the arc
made by a street lamp, and move on
to selfish futures,
our footsteps echoing in the dark
street have, for their companion,
his shadow with us.

Autumn is when small wars begin
drunken offensives; the skies spin
with reeling scanners;
but you, who left each feast at nine,
knew war, like free verse, is a sign
of awful manners.

Tonight, as every dish deploys
from sonar peaks its amplified
fireside oration,
we keep yours to ourselves, a voice
internal, intricately wired
as our salvation.

  II

In your flat world of silence
the fissures made by speech
close. A sandpiper signs
the margin of a beach.

Soon, from the whistling tundras,
geese following earth's arc
will find an accurate Indies
in the lime-scented dark.

Our conjugations, Master,
are still based on the beat
of wings that gave their cast to
our cuneiform alphabet,

though shredders hum with rage through
the neon afternoon,
and dials guide earth's marriage
to an irascible moon;

not needling Arcturus,
nor Saturn's visible hum
have, on their disks, a chorus
of epithalamium;

the farther the space station
from the Newtonian shelf,
the more man's conversation,
increases with himself.

Once, past a wooden vestry,
down still colonial streets,
the hoisted chords of Wesley
were strong as miners' throats;

in treachery and in union,
despite your Empire's wrong,
I made my first communion
there, with the English tongue.

It was such dispossession
that made possession joy,
when, strict as Psalm or Lesson,
I learnt your poetry.

### III

Twilight. Grey pigeons batten
on St. Mark's slate. A face
startles us with its pattern
of sunlit fire escapes.

Your slippered shadow pities
the railings where it moves,
brightening with *Nunc Dimittis*
the city it still loves.

O craft, that strangely chooses
one mouth to speak for all,
O Light no dark refuses,
O Space impenetrable,

fix, among constellations,
the spark we honour here,
whose planetary patience
repeats his earthly prayer

that the City may be Just,
and humankind be kind.
A barge moves, caked with rust
in the East River wind,

and the mouths of all the rivers
are still, and the estuaries
shine with the wake that gives the
craftsman the gift of peace.

■

# ETHERIDGE KNIGHT

## (1931–1991)

*The poems of Etheridge Knight often emerge from the margins of American society—prison, drug abuse, rural and urban poverty—that are not often represented in American literature. At its best, Mr. Knight's work is wise and lyrical, as well as sly, filled with a knowingness about the daily lives of blacks and how they live in society that can be both uproariously humorous and painfully true. Etheridge Knight was born in Mississippi and was badly wounded in the Korean War, an experience that he later attributed as the beginning of a downward spiral into drugs and crime. This activity culminated in a conviction and six-year prison term for armed robbery. While in prison he began writing poetry, which was later published to acclaim in the volume* Poems from Prison. *He died of cancer in 1991.*

## HARD ROCK RETURNS TO PRISON FROM THE HOSPITAL FOR THE CRIMINAL INSANE

Hard Rock / was / "known not to take no shit
From nobody," and he had the scars to prove it:
Split purple lips, lumbed ears, welts above
His yellow eyes, and one long scar that cut
Across his temple and plowed through a thick
Canopy of kinky hair.

The WORD / was / that Hard Rock wasn't a mean nigger
Anymore, that the doctors had bored a hole in his head,
Cut out part of his brain, and shot electricity
Through the rest. When they brought Hard Rock back,
Handcuffed and chained, he was turned loose,
Like a freshly gelded stallion, to try his new status.
And we all waited and watched, like a herd of sheep,
To see if the WORD was true.

As we waited we wrapped ourselves in the cloak
Of his exploits: "Man, the last time, it took eight
Screws to put him in the Hole." "Yeah, remember when he
Smacked the captain with his dinner tray?" "He set
The record for time in the Hole—67 straight days!"
"Ol Hard Rock! man, that's one crazy nigger."
And then the jewel of a myth that Hard Rock had once bit
A screw on the thumb and poisoned him with syphilitic spit.

The testing came, to see if Hard Rock was really tame.
A hillbilly called him a black son of a bitch
And didn't lose his teeth, a screw who knew Hard Rock
From before shook him down and barked in his face.
And Hard Rock did *nothing*. Just grinned and looked silly,
His eyes empty like knot holes in a fence.

And even after we discovered that it took Hard Rock
Exactly 3 minutes to tell you his first name,
We told ourselves that he had just wised up,
Was being cool; but we could not fool ourselves for long,
And we turned away, our eyes on the ground. Crushed.

He had been our Destroyer, the doer of things
We dreamed of doing but could not bring ourselves to do,
The fears of years, like a biting whip,
Had cut deep bloody grooves
Across our backs.


## THE IDEA OF ANCESTRY

### I

Taped to the wall of my cell are 47 pictures: 47 black
faces: my father, mother, grandmothers (1 dead), grand
fathers (both dead), brothers, sisters, uncles, aunts,
cousins (1st & 2nd), nieces, and nephews. They stare
across the space at me sprawling on my bunk. I know
their dark eyes, they know mine. I know their style,
they know mine. I am all of them, they are all of me;
they are farmers, I am a thief, I am me, they are thee.

I have at one time or another been in love with my mother,
1 grandmother, 2 sisters, 2 aunts (1 went to the asylum),
and 5 cousins. I am now in love with a 7 yr old niece
(she sends me letters written in large block print, and
her picture is the only one that smiles at me).

I have the same name as 1 grandfather, 3 cousins, 3 nephews,
and 1 uncle. The uncle disappeared when he was 15, just took
off and caught a freight (they say). He's discussed each year
when the family has a reunion, he causes uneasiness in
the clan, he is an empty space. My father's mother, who is 93
and who keeps the Family Bible with everybody's birth dates
(and death dates) in it, always mentions him. There is no
place in her Bible for "whereabouts unknown."

### II

Each Fall the graves of my grandfathers call me, the brown
hills and red gullies of mississippi send out their electric
messages, galvanizing my genes. Last yr/like a salmon quitting
the cold ocean—leaping and bucking up his birthstream/I
hitchhiked my way from L.A. with 16 caps in my pocket and a
monkey on my back, and I almost kicked it with the kinfolks.

I walked barefoot in my grandmother's backyard/I smelled the old
land and the woods/I sipped cornwhiskey from fruit jars with the
    men/
I flirted with the women/I had a ball till the caps ran out
and my habit came down. That night I looked at my grandmother
and split/my guts were screaming for junk/but I was almost
contented/I had almost caught up with me.
    The next day in Memphis I cracked a croaker's crib for a fix.

This yr there is a gray stone wall damming my stream, and when
the falling leaves stir my genes, I pace my cell or flop on my bunk
and stare at 47 black faces across the space. I am all of them,
they are all of me, I am me, they are thee, and I have no sons
to float in the space between.


## HAIKU

### 1

Eastern guard tower
glints in sunset; convicts rest
like lizards on rocks.

### 2

The piano man
is stingy at 3 A.M.
his songs drop like plum.

### 3

Morning sun slants cell.
Drunks stagger like cripple flies
On jailhouse floor.

### 4

To write a blues song
is to regiment riots
and pluck gems from graves.

### 5

A bare pecan tree
slips a pencil shadow down
a moonlit snow slope.

6

The falling snow flakes
Cannot blunt the hard aches nor
Match the steel stillness.

7

Under moon shadows
A tall boy flashes knife and
Slices star bright ice.

8

In the August grass
Struck by the last rays of sun
The cracked teacup screams.

9

Making jazz swing in
Seventeen syllables AIN'T
No square poet's job.


## FOR FRECKLE-FACED GERALD

Now you take ol Rufus. He beat drums,
was free and funky under the arms,
fucked white girls, jumped off a bridge
(and thought nothing of the sacrilege),
he copped out— and he was over twenty-one.

Take Gerald. Sixteen years hadn't even done
a good job on his voice. He didn't even know
how to talk tough, or how to hide the glow
of life before he was thrown in as "pigmeat"
for the buzzards to eat.

Gerald, who had no memory or hope of copper hot lips—
of firm upthrusting thighs
to reinforce his flow,
let tall walls and buzzards change the course
of his river from south to north.

(No safety in numbers, like back on the block:
two's aplenty. three? definitely not.
four? "you're all muslims."
five? "you were planning a race riot."
plus, Gerald could never quite win
with his precise speech and innocent grin
the trust and fists of the young black cats.)

Gerald, sun-kissed ten thousand times on the nose
and cheeks, didn't stand a chance,
didn't even know that the loss of his balls
had been plotted years in advance
by wiser and bigger buzzards than those
who now hover above his track
and at night light upon his back.

## A POEM FOR BLACK RELOCATION CENTERS

Flukum couldn't stand the strain. Flukum
wanted inner and outer order, so
he joined the army where U.S. Manuals made
everything plain—even how to button his shirt,
and how to kill yellow men. (If Flukum
ever felt hurt or doubt about who his enemy
was, the Troop Information Officer or the Stars
and Stripes straightened him out.)
And, we must not forget
that Flukum was paid well to let the Red
Blood. And sin? If Flukum ever thought about sin
or Hell for squashing the yellow men, the good Chaplain
(Holy by God and by Congress) pointed out with
Devilish skill that to kill the colored men was not
altogether a sin.

Flukum marched back from the war, straight and tall,
and with presents for all: a water pipe for daddy,
teeny teacups for mama, sheer silk for tittee, and
a jade inlaid dagger for me. But, with a smile
on his face in a place just across the bay,
Flukum, the patriot, got shot that same day,
got shot in his great wide chest, bedecked with good
conduct ribbons. He died surprised, he had thought
the enemy far away on the other side of the sea.


## DARK PROPHECY: I SING OF SHINE

And, yeah, brothers
while white / america sings about the unsink-
able molly brown
(who was hustling the titanic
when it went down)
I sing to thee of Shine
the stoker who was hip enough to flee the fucking ship
and let the white folks drown
with screams on their lips
(jumped his black ass into the dark sea, Shine did,
broke free from the straining steel).
Yeah, I sing to thee of Shine
and how the millionaire banker stood on the deck
and pulled from his pockets a million dollar check
saying Shine Shine save poor me
and I'll give you all the money a black boy needs—
how Shine looked at the money and then at the sea
and said jump in mothafucka and swim like me—
And Shine swam on—Shine swam on—
and how the banker's daughter ran naked on the deck
with her pink tits trembling and her pants roun her neck
screaming Shine Shine save poor me
and I'll give you all the pussy a black boy needs—
how Shine said now pussy is good and that's no jive
but you got to swim not fuck to stay alive—
And Shine swam on Shine swam on—

How Shine swam past a preacher afloating on a board
crying save *me* nigger Shine in the name of the Lord—
and how the preacher grabbed Shine's arm and broke his stroke—
how Shine pulled his shank and cut the preacher's throat—
And Shine swam on—Shine swam on—
And when the news hit shore that the titanic had sunk
Shine was up in Harlem damn near drunk

# GERALD BARRAX

## (B. 1933)

*Gerald Barrax is the author of fragile and delicate lyric poems that often are concerned with the perceptions of a man trying to make his way through today's difficult and unseemly world while trying to remain true to himself and his best impulses. Influenced by fellow Baha'i Robert Hayden, among others, Mr. Barrax writes poems that at their best can be both tender and startling. Gerald Barrax was born in Attalla, Alabama, and grew up there and in Pittsburgh. He studied at Duquesne University, the University of Pittsburgh, and the University of North Carolina, and is professor of English at North Carolina State University. The author of four books of poems, he lives in Raleigh with his family.*

## LAST LETTER

I might not have known his voice
And he would have known mine
As one-too-many wrong numbers
Except grief had deafened him
As your silence had terrified me of discoveries
As one day and another
And another had gone and no letter
No call came.

We were so good, so clever
We needed no third friend,
We had no one to tell me,
Who had no rights in your life.
He didn't say you were dead:
You were buried "just yesterday, just
Yesterday."
That deep trough in your back.
The small crease between your eyes.


## KING: APRIL 4, 1968

*For Eva Ray*

When I was a child
in the Fall the axes fell
in Alabama and I tried
to be somewhere else,
but the squeals of the pigs dying
and hogs and the sight of their
opened throats were everywhere.

I wasn't given that kind of stomach.

When I was 14 I killed
the last thing bigger than a mouse
with my Daisy Red Ryder:
a fat robin on a telephone wire,
still singing,
as my first shot went high
I sighted down and HEARD from where I was
the soft thud of the copper pellet in his
fat red breast. It just stopped
and fell over backwards
and I had run away
before it hit the ground, taking
my stomach with me.

I'll never know about people—
if the soft thing in the gut can be cut out—
because I missed all the wars—
but when I learned that non
violence kills you anyway
I wished
I wished I could do it I wished I
could
do you know what it means to wish
you could kill, to
wish you were given that?

But I am
me. Whatever made me made
you, and I anesthetize the soft thing
to stop squirming when
you do it brothers I shout
righton, righton, rightON
my heart is with you
though my stomach is still in Alabama pig
pens.


## THE SINGER

> *for Nina, Roberta, Aretha.*
> *Sarah, Ella, Carmen.*
> *Dinah, Billie, Bessie. And Ma.*

Black Angel
Doing what she's gotta do
The sister sings

"Like a stone bird"
He said, intending to praise her.
But no bird has such a choice.

They speak, too,
Or whatever twittering means
But does that explain human song?

Maybe this more than natural impulse
Surprised even the creator
Who let the possibility

Slip his mind.
Not unintended.
Just not thought of.

  Suppose
There was a creature
not yet human
who cocked his head, dimly quizzical
at birdsong
and did something—
roared, screeched, howled—
something purely joyous in imitation
and those birds filled the prehistoric air
in flight from his obscenity.

Who was to tell him
he wasn't created for that? Or
      suppose Eve.
Giving a name
to something dull Adam
didn't know about:

      *What's that? What are you doing?*

And she, holding the doomed child,
stopped and looked at him as if listening
and smiled, and said

      *Singing.*

Not like birds
Who are doomed to sing
Her doom and ours is her silence.
      The sisters sing
      Doing what they've gotta do
      Black Angels

# SONIA SANCHEZ
## (B. 1934)

*Sonia Sanchez has had a widely varied career as a poet, teacher, lecturer, and commentator. She is one of the best poets to emerge from the Black Arts Movement of the late sixties and early seventies, and her work has continued to expand and deepen in the time since. Her representative poems are both baldly honest and moving. Ms. Sanchez is often described as a political poet, and by any definition she is; it is, however, when that political voice merges with her own personal, lyric voice that Ms. Sanchez's work searingly narrates the passions and concerns of an astute and aware black woman in the late twentieth century. Finally, Ms. Sanchez is also capable of lyric poems of distilled purity and pain, which harken back to her graduate studies with Louise Bogan. Sonia Sanchez was born in Birmingham, Alabama, and moved at an early age to New York City. A graduate of Hunter College, she is currently professor of African-American Studies at Temple University in Philadelphia.*

## PERSONAL LETTER NO. 3

nothing will keep
us young you know
not young men or
women who spin
their youth on
cool playing sounds.
we are what we
are what we never
think we are.
no more wild geo
graphies of the
flesh. echoes. that
we move in tune
to slower smells.

it is a hard thing
to admit that
sometimes after midnight
i am tired
of it all.


## REFLECTIONS AFTER THE JUNE 12TH MARCH FOR DISARMAMENT

I have come to you tonite out of the depths
   of slavery
   from white hands peeling black skins over
   america;
I have come out to you from reconstruction eyes
   that closed on black humanity
   that reduced black hope to the dark
   huts of america;
I have come to you from the lynching years,
   the exploitation of black men and women by
   a country that allowed the swinging of
   strange fruits from southern trees;
I have come to you tonite thru the
   delaney years, the du bois years, the
   b.t. washington years, the robeson
   years, the garvey years, the
   depression years, the you can't eat
   or sit or live just die here years,
   the civil rights years, the black power
   years, the black nationalist years, the
   affirmative action years, the liberal
   years, the neo-conservative years;
I have come to say that those years
   were not in vain, the ghosts of our
   ancestors searching this american dust for
   rest were not in vain, black women
   walking their lives in clots were not
   in vain, the years walked
   sideways in a forsaken land were not
   in vain;

I have come to you tonite as an equal,
  as a comrade, as a black woman
  walking down a corridor of tears,
  looking neither to the left or the right,
  pulling my history with bruised
  heels,
  beckoning to the illusion of america
  daring you to look me in the eyes to
  see these faces, the exploitation of a
  people because of skin pigmentation;
I have come to you tonite because no people
  have been asked to be modern day people
  with the history of slavery, and still
  we walk, and still we talk, and
  still we plan, and still we hope and
  still we sing;
I have come to you tonite because there are
  inhumanitarians in the world. they are not
  new. they are old. they go back into history.
  they were called explorers, soldiers, mercenaries,
  imperialists, missionaries, adventurers,
  but they looked at the world for what
  it would give up to them and they violated
  the land and the people, they looked
  at the land and sectioned it up for
  private ownership, they looked at the
  people and decided how to manipulate
  them thru fear and ignorance, they looked
  at the gold and began to hoard and
  worship it;
I have come to you because it is time
  for us all to purge capitalism from
  our dreams, to purge materialism
  from our eyes, from the planet earth
  to deliver the earth again into the hands
  of the humanitarians;
I have come to you tonite not just for the stoppage
  of nuclear proliferation, nuclear
  plants, nuclear bombs, nuclear
  waste, but to stop the proliferation
  of nuclear minds, of nuclear generals
  of nuclear presidents, of nuclear scientists,

who spread human and nuclear waste
over the world;
I come to you because the world needs to be
saved for the future generations who must
return the earth to peace, who will not
be startled by a man's/woman's skin color;
I come to you because the world needs sanity
now, needs men and women who will
not work to produce nuclear weapons,
who will give up their need for excess
wealth and learn how to share the
world's resources, who will never
again as scientists invent again just
for the sake of inventing;
I come to you because we need to turn our
eyes to the beauty of this planet, to the
bright green laughter of trees, to the beautiful
human animals waiting to smile their unprostituted smiles;
I have come to you to talk about our inexperience
at living as human beings, thru death marches and camps,
thru middle passages and slavery
and thundering countries raining hungry faces;
I am here to move against
leaving our shadows implanted on the
earth while our bodies disintegrate in
nuclear lightning;
I am here between the voices of our ancestors
and the noise of the planet,
between the surprise of death and life;
I am here because I shall not give the
earth up to non-dreamers and earth molesters;
I am here to say to you:
my body is full of veins
like the bombs waiting to burst
with blood.
we must learn to suckle life not
bombs and rhetoric
rising up in redwhiteandblue patriotism;
I am here. and my breath/our breaths
must thunder across this land
arousing new breaths. new life.
new people, who will live in peace
and honor.

# DEPRESSION

### 1

i have gone into my eyes
bumping against sockets that sing
smelling the evening from under the sun
where waterless bones move
toward their rivers in incense.
a piece of light crawls up and down
then turns a corner.

as when drunken air molts in beds,
tumbling over blankets that cover sweat
nudging into sheets continuing dreams;
so i have settled in wheelbarrows
grotesque with wounds,
small and insistent as sleigh bells.

am i a voice delighting in the sand?
look how the masks rock on the winds
moving in tune to leaves.
i shed my clothes.
am i a seed consumed by breasts
without the weasel's eye
or the spaniel teeth of a child?

### 2

i have cried all night
tears pouring out of my forehead
sluggish in pulse,
tears from a spinal soul
that run in silence to my birth
ayyyy! am i born? i cannot peel the flesh.
i hear the moon daring
to dance these rooms.
O to become a star.
stars seek their own mercy
and sigh the quiet, like gods.

# elegy
## (for MOVE* and Philadelphia)

1.

philadelphia
   a disguised southern city
squatting in the eastern pass of
colleges cathedrals and cowboys.
philadelphia. a phalanx of parsons
and auctioneers
   modern gladiators
erasing the delirium of death from their shields
while houses burn out of control.

2.

c'mon girl hurry on down to osage st
they're roasting in the fire
smell the dreadlocks and blk/skins
roasting in the fire.

c'mon newsmen and tvmen
hurryondown to osage st and
when you have chloroformed the city
and after you have stitched up your words
hurry on downtown for sanctuary
in taverns and corporations

and the blood is not yet dry.

3.

how does one scream in thunder?

4.

they are combing the morning for shadows
and screams tongue-tied without faces
look. over there. one eye
escaping from its skin
and our heartbeats slowdown to a drawl
and the kingfisher calls out from his downtown capital
And the pinstriped general reenlists
his tongue for combat
and the police come like twin seasons of drought and flood.
they're combing the city for lifeliberty and
the pursuit of happiness.

5.

how does one city scream in thunder?

6.

hide us O lord
deliver us from our nakedness.
exile us from our laughter
give us this day our rest from seduction
peeling us down to our veins.

and the tower was like no other.                    amen.
and the streets escaped under the
cover of darkness                                    amen.
and the voices called out from
their wounds                                         amen.
and the fire circumcised the city                    amen.

7.

who anointeth this city with napalm?                 (i say)
who giveth this city in holy infanticide?

8.

beyond the mornings and afternoons
and deaths detonating the city.
beyond the tourist roadhouses
trading in lobotomies
there is a glimpse of earth
this prodigal earth.
beyond edicts and commandments
commissioned by puritans
there are people
navigating the breath of hurricanes.
beyond concerts and football
and mummers strutting their
sequined processionals.
there is this earth. this country. this city.
this people.
collecting skeletons from waiting rooms
lying in wait. for honor and peace.
one day.

*MOVE: a Philadelphia based back to nature group whose headquarters was bombed by
the police on May 13, 1985, killing men, women and children. An entire city block was
destroyed by fire.

# PHILADELPHIA: SPRING, 1985

### 1.

*/a phila. fireman reflects after
seeing a decapitated body in the MOVE ruins/*

to see those eyes
orange like butterflies
over the walls.

i must move away
from this little-ease
where the pulse
shrinks into itself
and carve myself in white.

O to press the seasons
and taste the quiet juice
of their veins.

### 2. */memory/*

a.

Thus in the varicose town
where eyes splintered the night with glass
the children touched at random
sat in places where legions rode.

And O we watched the young birds
stretch the sky
until it streamed white ashes
and O we saw mountains lean on seas
to drink the blood of whales
then wander dumb with their wet bowels.

b.

Everywhere young
faces breathing in crusts.
breakfast of dreams.
The city, lit by a single fire,
followed the air into disorder.
And the sabbath stones singed our eyes
with each morning's coin.

c.

Praise of a cureless death they heard
without confessor;
Praise of cathedrals
pressing their genesis from priests;
Praise of wild gulls who came and drank
their summer's milk,
then led them toward the parish snow.

How still the spiderless city.
The earth is immemorial in death.

# IMAMU AMIRI BARAKA

## (B. 1934)

*Amiri Baraka was born Leroi Jones in Newark, New Jersey. His personal odyssey can be seen to mirror that of African Americans in the United States since World War II. Mr. Baraka was a very talented youngster, writing and drawing at a young age, graduating early from high school, attending college (Howard University), and serving in the Air Force. After graduate study at Columbia University, he became a quick success on the New York literary scene, publishing poetry and editing a magazine. His play Dutchman was very popular off-Broadway. In the mid-sixties, a growing disenchantment with American society as a whole coalesced in Mr. Baraka as a rejection of white America and any hopes he had harbored of building a truly multi-racial nation. Mr. Baraka then focused his artistic efforts in and on the black community and became an active and adept politician as well. He has described his evolving position: "To understand that you are black in a society where black is an extreme liability is one thing, but to understand that it is the society that is lacking and impossibly deformed, and not yourself, isolates you even more." The poetry of Amiri Baraka can be by turns tender, angry, and funny, written in many different styles, tones, and techniques. It is a window into the rage of some mid-century blacks, particularly those of urban ghettoes, who have watched several social "movements" come and go without much substantive change. Mr. Baraka is the author of many books of poetry, criticism, and fiction as well as plays. He is currently a professor at the State University of New York at Stony Brook.*

## PREFACE TO A TWENTY VOLUME SUICIDE NOTE

*(For Kellie Jones, born 16 May 1959)*

Lately, I've become accustomed to the way
The ground opens up and envelops me
Each time I go out to walk the dog.
Or the broad edged silly music the wind
Makes when I run for a bus . . .

Things have come to that.

And now, each night I count the stars,
And each night I get the same number.
And when they will not come to be counted,
I count the holes they leave.

Nobody sings anymore.

And then last night, I tiptoed up
To my daughter's room and heard her
Talking to someone, and when I opened
The door, there was no one there . . .
Only she on her knees, peeking into

Her own clasped hands.


## *FROM* HYMN TO LANIE POO: EACH MORNING

4

Each morning
I go down
to Gansevoort St.
and stand on the docks.

I stare out
at the horizon
until it gets up
and comes to embrace
me. I
make believe
it is my father.
This is known
as genealogy.

## SHORT SPEECH TO MY FRIENDS

A political art, let it be
tenderness, low strings the fingers
touch, or the width of autumn
climbing wider avenues, among the virtue
and dignity of knowing what city
you're in, who to talk to, what clothes
—even what buttons—to wear. I address

/the society
the image, of
common utopia.
/The perversity
of separation, isolation,
after so many years of trying to enter their kingdoms,
now they suffer in tears, these others, saxophones whining
through the wooden doors of their less than gracious homes.
The poor have become our creators. The black. The thoroughly
ignorant.
Let the combination of morality
and inhumanity
begin.

2.

Is power, the enemy? (Destroyer
of dawns, cool flesh of valentines, among
the radios, pauses, drunks
of the 19th century. I see it,
as any man's single history. All the possible heroes
dead from heat exhaustion

at the beach,
or hiding for years from cameras
only to die cheaply in the pages
of our daily lie.
One hero
has pretensions toward literature
one toward the cultivation of errors, arrogance,
and constantly changing disguises, as trucker, boxer,
valet, barkeep, in the ageing taverns of memory. Making love
to those speedy heroines of masturbation. Or kicking literal evil
continually down filmy public stairs.


A compromise
would be silence. To shut up, even such risk
as the proper placement
of verbs and nouns. To freeze the spit
in mid-air, as it aims itself
at some valiant intellectual's face.
There would be someone
who would understand, for whatever
fancy reason. Dead, lying, Roi, as your children
came up, would also rise. As George Armstrong Custer
these 100 years, has never made
a mistake.




## THREE MODES OF HISTORY AND CULTURE


Chalk mark sex of the nation, on walls we drummers
know
as cathedrals. Cathedra, in a churning meat milk.


Women glide through looking for telephones. Maps
weep
and are mothers and their daughters listening to


music teachers. From heavy beginnings. Plantations,
learning
America, as speech, and a common emptiness. Songs knocking

inside old women's faces. Knocking through cardboard trunks.
Trains
leaning north, catching hellfire in windows, passing through

the first ignoble cities of missouri, to illinois, and the panting
Chicago.
And then all ways, we go where flesh is cheap. Where factories

sit open, burning the chiefs. Make your way! Up through fog and
history
Make your way, and swing the general, that it come flash open

and spill the innards of that sweet thing we heard, and gave theory
to.
Breech, bridge, and reach, to where all talk is energy. And there's

enough, for anything singular. All our lean prophets and rhythms.
Entire
we arrive and set up shacks, hole cards, Western hearts at the edge

of saying. Thriving to balance the meanness of particular skies.
Race
of madmen and giants.

Brick songs. Shoe songs. Chants of open weariness.
Knife wiggle early evenings of the wet mouth. Tongue
dance midnight, any season shakes our house. Don't
tear my clothes! To doubt the balance of misery

ripping meat hug shuffle fuck. The Party of Insane
Hope, I've come from there too. Where the dead told lies
about clever social justice. Burning coffins voted
and staggered through cold white streets listening
to Willkie or Wallace or Dewey through the dead face
of Lincoln. Come from there, and belched it out.

I think about a time when I will be relaxed.
When flames and non-specific passion wear themselves
away. And my eyes and hands and mind can turn
and soften, and my songs will be softer
and lightly weight the air.

## BLACK ART

Poems are bullshit unless they are
teeth or trees or lemons piled
on a step. Or black ladies dying
of men leaving nickel hearts
beating them down. Fuck poems
and they are useful, wd they shoot
come at you, love what you are,
breathe like wrestlers, or shudder
strangely after pissing. We want live
words of the hip world live flesh &
coursing blood. Hearts Brains
Souls splintering fire. We want poems
like fists beating niggers out of Jocks
or dagger poems in the slimy bellies
of the owner-jews. Black poems to
smear on girdlemamma mulatto bitches
whose brains are red jelly stuck
between 'lizabeth taylor's toes. Stinking
Whores! We want "poems that kill."
Assassin poems, Poems that shoot
guns. Poems that wrestle cops into alleys
and take their weapons leaving them dead
with tongues pulled out and sent to Ireland. Knockoff
poems for dope selling wops or slick halfwhite
politicians Airplane poems, rrrrrrrrrrrrrrrr
rrrrrrrrrrrrrrr . . . tuhtuhtuhtuhtuhtuhtuhtuhtuh
. . . rrrrrrrrrrrrrrr . . . Setting fire and death to
whities ass. Look at the Liberal
Spokesman for the jews clutch his throat
& puke himself into eternity . . . rrrrrrrr
There's a negroleader pinned to
a bar stool in Sardi's eyeballs melting
in hot flame Another negroleader
on the steps of the white house one
kneeling between the sheriff's thighs
negotiating coolly for his people.
Agggh . . . stumbles across the room . . .
Put it on him, poem. Strip him naked
to the world! Another bad poem cracking

steel knuckles in a jewlady's mouth
Poem scream poison gas on beasts in green berets
Clean out the world for virtue and love,
Let there be no love poems written
until love can exist freely and
cleanly. Let Black People understand
that they are the lovers and the sons
of lovers and warriors and sons
of warriors Are poems & poets &
all the loveliness here in the world

We want a black poem. And a
Black World.
Let the world be a Black Poem
And Let All Black People Speak This Poem
Silently
or LOUD

## BLACK BOURGEOISIE,

has a gold tooth, sits long hours
on a stool thinking about money.
sees white skin in a secret room
rummages his sense for sense
dreams about Lincoln (s)
conks his daughter's hair
sends his coon to school
works very hard
grins politely in restaurants
has a good word to say
never says it
does not hate ofays
hates, instead, him self
him black self

## CLAY

Killed
by a white woman
on a subway
in 1964.
he rose
>to be the first negro congressman
>from missouri.
>we're not saying
>that being dead
>is the pre
>requisite
>for this honor
>but it certainly helped make him
>what he is
>today.

# AUDRE LORDE

## (1934–1992)

*"It's easier to deal with a poet," Audre Lorde said in an interview,*
*"certainly a Black woman poet, when you can categorize her, narrow*
*her so she can fulfill your expectations." Lorde spent significant por-*
*tions of her artistic and political lives dodging and shucking those ex-*
*pectations, writing deeply and variously as a woman, a black person,*
*a lesbian, a politically aware New Yorker, and any combination of*
*these and other aspects of her personality. She was born in Harlem to*
*Caribbean immigrants, and her poems can be seen as documenting*
*her journey through societally imposed roles—black, wife, teacher—*
*toward her own authentic choices as poet, feminist, lesbian, and be-*
*yond. These labels and choices are not necessarily simple; much of her*
*work is concerned with the inefficacy of our usual ways of describing,*
*and with such paradoxes as how knowing more of her personal and*
*historical black self helped her emerge more fully into the wider*
*world. Audre Lorde graduated from Hunter College, received an MLS*
*from Columbia University, and worked as a librarian and school-*
*teacher before becoming professor of English at Hunter College in*
*1981. She died of cancer in 1992.*

## COAL

I   is the total black
being spoken
from the earth's inside.

There are many kinds of open
how a diamond comes
into a knot of flame
how sound comes into a word
colored
by who pays what for speaking.

Some words are open
diamonds on a glass window
singing out within the crash
of passing sun
other words are stapled wagers
in a perforated book
buy and sign and tear apart
and come whatever wills all chances
the stub remains
an ill-pulled tooth
with a ragged edge.

Some words live in my throat
breeding like adders
others
know sun
seeking like gypsies
over my tongue
to explode through my lips
like young sparrows
bursting from shell.

Some words
bedevil me.

Love is a word, another kind of open.
As the diamond comes
into a knot of flame
I am Black
because I come from the earth's inside
take my word for jewel
in the open light.

(1962)

## PROLOGUE

Haunted by poems beginning with I
seek out those whom I love who are deaf
to whatever does not destroy
or curse the old ways that did not serve us
while history falters and our poets are dying
choked into silence by icy distinction
death rattles blind curses
and I hear even my own voice becoming
a pale strident whisper
At night sleep locks me into an echoless coffin
sometimes at noon I dream
there is nothing to fear
now standing up in the light of my father sun
without shadow
I speak without concern for the accusations
that I am too much or too little woman
that I am too Black or too white
or too much myself
and through my lips come the voices
of the ghosts of our ancestors
living and moving among us.

Hear my heart's voice as it darkens
pulling old rhythms out of the earth
that will receive this piece of me
and a piece of each one of you
when our part in history quickens again
and is over:

Hear
the old ways are going away
and coming back pretending change
masked as denunciation and lament
masked as a choice
between an eager mirror that blurs and distorts us
in easy definitions    until our image
shatters along its fault
or the other half of that choice
speaking to our hidden fears with a promise
our eyes need not seek any truer shape—
a face at high noon particular and unadorned—
for we have learned to fear
the light from clear water might destroy us
with reflected emptiness or a face without tongue
with no love or with terrible penalties
for any difference
and even as I speak remembered pain is moving
shadows over my face, my own voice fades and
my brothers and sisters are leaving;

Yet when I was a child
whatever my mother thought would mean survival
made her try to beat me whiter every day
and even now the color of her bleached ambition
still forks throughout my words
but I survived
and didn't I survive    confirmed
to teach my children where her errors lay
etched across their faces between the kisses
that she pinned me with asleep
and my mother beating me
as white as snow melts in the sunlight
loving me into her bloods black bone—
the home of all her secret hopes and fears
and my dead father whose great hands
weakened in my judgment
whose image broke inside of me
beneath the weight of failure
helps me to know who I am not
weak or mistaken
my father loved me alive

to grow and hate him
and now his grave voice joins hers
within my words    rising and falling
are my sisters and brothers listening?

The children remain
like blades of grass over the earth and
all the children are singing
louder than mourning
all their different voices
sound like a raucous question
they do not fear empty mirrors
they have seen their faces defined in a hydrant's puddle
before the rainbows of oil obscured them.
The time of lamentation and curses is passing.

My mother survives
through more than chance or token.
Although she will read what I write
with embarrassment    or anger
and a small understanding
my children do not need to relive my past
in strength nor in confusion
nor care that their holy fires
may destroy
more than my failures.

Somewhere in the landscape past noon
I shall leave a dark print of the me that I am
and who I am not
etched in a shadow
of angry and remembered loving
and their ghosts will move
whispering through them
with me none the wiser
for they will have buried me
either in shame
or in peace.

And the grasses will still be
Singing.

# FATHER SON AND HOLY GHOST

I have not ever seen my father's grave.

Not that his judgment eyes
have been forgotten
nor his great hands' print
on our evening doorknobs
        one half turn each night
        and he would come
        drabbled with the world's business
        massive and silent
        as the whole day's wish
        ready to redefine
        each of our shapes
but now the evening doorknobs
wait    and do not recognize us
as we pass.

Each week a different woman
regular as his one quick glass
each evening
pulls up the grass his stillness grows
calling it weed.
Each week    a different woman
has my mother's face
and he
who time has    changeless
must be amazed
who knew and loved
but one.

My father died in silence
loving creation
and well-defined response
He lived    still judgments
on familiar things
and died    knowing
a January 15th that year me.

Lest I go into dust
I have not ever seen my father's grave.

(1960)

# FOR THE RECORD

*in memory of Eleanor Bumpers*

Call out the colored girls
and the ones who call themselves Black
and the ones who hate the word nigger
and the ones who are very pale

Who will count the big fleshy women
the grandmother weighing 22 stone
with the rusty braids
and a gap-toothed scowl
who wasn't afraid of Armageddon
the first shotgun blast tore her right arm off
the one with the butcher knife
the second blew out her heart
through the back of her chest
and I am going to keep writing it down
how they carried her body out of the house
dress torn    up around her waist
uncovered
past tenants and the neighborhood children
a mountain of Black Woman
and I am going to keep telling this
if it kills me
and it might in ways I am
learning

The next day Indira Gandhi
was shot down in her garden
and I wonder what these two 67-year-old
colored girls
are saying to each other now
planning their return
and they weren't even
sisters.

## BEAMS

In the afternoon sun
that smelled of contradiction
quick birds announcing spring's intention
and autumn about to begin
I started to tell you
what Eudora never told me
how quickly it goes
the other fork    out of mind's eye
choice
becoming a stone wall
across possible
beams
outlined on the shapes of winter
the sunset colors of Southampton Beach
red-snapper runs at Salina Cruz
and we slept in the fishermen's nets
a pendulum swing
between the rippling fingers
of a belly dancer with brass rings
and a two-year-old's sleep smell
the inexorable dwindling
no body's choice
and for a few short summers
I too was delightful.

Whenever spring comes I wish to burn
to ride the flood like a zebra goaded
shaken with sun
to braid the hair of a girl long dead
or is it my daughter grown
and desire for what is gone
sealed into hunger    like an abandoned mine
nights when fear came down like a jones
and I lay    rigid with denials
the clarity of frost without
the pain of coldness
autumn's sharp precisions and yet
for the green to stay.

Dark women clad in flat and functional leather
finger their breastsummers   whispering
sisterly advice   one dreams of fish
lays her lips like spring across my chest
where I am scarred and naked
as a strip-mined hill in West Virginia
and hanging on my office wall
a snapshot of the last Dahomean Amazons
taken the year that I was born
three old Black women in draped cloths
holding hands.

A knout of revelation   a corm of song
and love   a net of possible
surrounding all acts of life
one woman harvesting   all I have ever been
lights up my sky like stars
or flecks of paint   storm-flung
the blast and seep of gone
remains
only the peace we make with it
shifts into seasons
lengthening past equinox
sun   wind   come round again
seizing us in her arms like a warrior lover
or blowing us into shapes
we have avoided for years
as we turn
we forget what is not possible.

A *jones:* a drug habit or addiction.
*Breastsummer:* a breastplate; also a wooden beam across an empty place.

# JAY WRIGHT

## (B. 1935)

In his poems, Jay Wright takes the broadest possible view of the
American landscape as he narrates one soul's journey through it. He
writes from an ever-shifting complex of viewpoints, American (Afri-
can, native, western), West African, and Latin American, weaving
them all into a profound and original perspective on North American
history and culture. Mr. Wright himself has said that these varying
strands of his work are already woven, and that his art is simply an
attempt to "uncover the weave." These poems can range, in subject
matter, from the lament of a failed jazz musician to the remembrance
of a cemetery in Mr. Wright's childhood New Mexico to a meditation
on death and regeneration utilizing the symbols and cosmology of
West African religion. Jay Wright has been influenced by an eclectic
mix of writers and thinkers, including Robert Hayden, W. E. B. Du-
Bois, Benjamin Banneker, Ralph Ellison, Hart Crane, Rainer Maria
Rilke, Dante, and Wole Soyinka. In the manner of Robert Hayden,
what Mr. Wright makes of all this might be concentrated into a short
and perfect lyric, or expanded over a multipart epic filled with his-
tory, found materials, and dense narration. His is a unique vision,
and promises to be one of the few that attempt to encompass the
continent. Jay Wright was born in Albuquerque, New Mexico, was
educated at the University of California at Berkeley and Rutgers Uni-
versity, and has held Guggenheim and MacArthur fellowships, among
others. The author of nine books of poems, he lives in New Hampshire.


## DEATH AS HISTORY

### I

They are all dying,
all the ones who make
living worth the price,
and there is hardly time

to lament the passing
of their historical necessity.
Young poets sit in their rooms
like perverted Penelopes,
unraveling everything,
kicking the threads
into the wind,
and I stop,
woolly-eyed,
trying to record
this peculiar American game.
But they are dying,
the living ones,
and I am sapped of all resolve,
fleeced, finally, of the skill
to live among these others.
To be charged with so much living
is such an improbability,
to be improbable about living
is such a charge to hold
against oneself,
against those who are dying.

II

Dropping his history books,
a young man, lined against the horizon
like an exclamation point with nothing to assert,
stumbles into the dance.
The dancers go round and round
like drones on an unhappy flight.
They look to him for another possibility.
They hum.
They plead.
They circle him with outstretched hands.
They offer him their own salvation.
And he moves forward with a rose.
All that long search
to bring back death.
Who wants that old mystery?

### III

But still there is the probable.
And even in Madrid
the golden ages settle
in their sturdy coffins.
Oh, you can say that there
where the olive trees burst up
through the asphalt cells,
where well-endowed bulls butt
the tail-end of tame Sundays,
and coquettish river flings
its hips at the cattle-mouthed mountains.
Everything there is an imitation.
The girls always advance on the square,
repeating the vital moments,
needing no bookish priests
to redeem that dance.
And it is always the credible dance.

### IV

It is always like the beginning.
It is always having the egg
and seven circles,
always casting about in the wind
on that particular spot;
it is that African myth
we use to challenge death.
What we learn is that
death is not complete in itself,
only the final going from self to self.

### V

And death is the reason
to begin again, without letting go.
And who can lament
such historical necessity?
If they are all dying,
the living ones,
they charge us with the improbable.

## AN INVITATION TO
## MADISON COUNTY

I ride through Queens,
out to International Airport,
on my way to Jackson, Tougaloo, Mississippi.
I take out a notebook,
write "my southern journal," and the date.
I write something,
but can't get down the apprehension,
the strangeness, the uncertainty
of zipping in over the Sunday streets,
with the bank clock flashing the weather
and time, as if it were a lighthouse
and the crab-like cars mistook it
for their own destination.
The air terminal looks
like a city walled in, waiting for war.
The arrivals go down to the basement,
recruits waking at five AM to check out their gear,
to be introduced to the business end of the camp.
Fifteen minutes in the city,
and nothing has happened.
No one has asked me to move over
for a small parade of pale women,
or called me nigger, or asked me where I'm from.
Sure only of my destination, I wait.

Now, we move out through the quiet city,
past clean brick supermarkets,
past clean brick houses with nameplates and bushy lawns,
past the sleepy-eyed travelers,
locked tightly in their cars.
No one speaks. The accent I've been
waiting to hear is still far off,
still only part of that apprehension
I had on the highway, in Queens.

The small campus springs up
out of the brown environment,
half-green, half-brown, covered over
with scaly white wooden houses.
It seems to be fighting this atmosphere,
fighting to bring some beauty
out of the dirt roads, the tense isolation of this place.
Out to Mama T's, where farmers, young instructors
and students scream for hamburgers and beer,
rub each other in the light of the jukebox,
and talk, and talk. I am still
not in Jackson, not in Mississippi,
still not off that highway in Queens,
nor totally out of Harlem, still
have not made it into this place,
where the tables creak, and the crickets
close up Sunday, just at evening,
and people are saying goodnight early.
Afraid now, I wonder how I'll get into it,
how I can make my hosts forget
these impatient gestures, the matching socks and tie.
I wonder how long I'll have to listen
to make them feel I listen, wonder
what I can say that will say,
"It's all right. I don't understand,
a thing. Let me meet you here, in your home.
Teach me what you know,
for I think I'm coming home."

Then I meet a teen-aged girl,
who knows that I can read.
I ride with her to Madison County,
up backroads that stretch
with half-fulfilled crops,
half-filled houses, half-satisfied
cows, and horses, and dogs.
She does all the talking,
challenging me to name the trees,
the plants, the cities in Mississippi, her dog.
We reach her house,
a shack dominated by an old stove,
with its smoky outline going up the wall

into the Mississippi air, mattresses tossed
around the table, where a small piece of cornbread
and a steaming plate of greens wait for her.
Her mother comes out, hands folded before her
like a madonna. She speaks to me,
moving step by step back into the house,
asking me to come again,
as if I were dismissed,
as if there were nothing more
that I could want from her, from Madison County,
no secret that I could ask her to repeat,
not even ask about the baby resting there on her belly,
nor if she ever knew anyone with my name
in Madison County, in Mississippi.

Since I can't, and will not, move,
she stays, with her head coming up,
finally, in a defiant smile.
She watches me sniff the greens,
look around at the bare trees
heaving up out of the bare ground.
She watches my surprise,
as I look at her manly nine-year-old
drive a tractor through the fields.
I think of how she is preparing him
for death, how one day he'll pack
whatever clothes remain from the generations,
and go off down the road,
her champion, her soldier, her lovable boy,
her grief, into Jackson, and away,
past that lighthouse clock,
past the sleepy streets,
and come up screaming,
perhaps on the highway in Queens,
thinking that he'll find me,
the poet with matching socks and tie,
who will tell him all about the city,
who will drink with him in a bar
where lives are crackling, with the smell
of muddy-rooted bare trees, half-sick cows
and simmering greens still in his nose.

But I'm still not here,
still can't ask an easy question,
or comment on the boy, the bright girl,
the open fields, the smell of the greens;
can't even say, yes, I remember this,
or heard of it, or want to know it;
can't apologize for my clean pages,
or assert that I must change, after being here;
can't say that I'm after spirits in Mississippi,
that I've given up my apprehension
about pale and neatly dressed couples
speeding past the lighthouse clock,
silently going home to their own apprehensions;
can't say, yes, you're what I really came for,
you, your scaly hands, your proud, surreptitious
smile, your commanding glance at your son,
that's what I do not search, but discover.

I stand in Madison County,
where you buy your clothes, your bread,
your very life, from hardline politicians,
where the inessential cotton still comes up
as if it were king, and belonged to you,
where the only escape is down that road,
with your slim baggage, into war,
into some other town that smells the same,
into a relative's crowded house
in some uncertain city, into the arms
of poets, who would be burned,
who would wake in the Mississippi rain,
listening for your apprehension,
standing at the window in different shadows,
finally able to say, "I don't understand.
But I would be taught your strength."

The father comes down the road,
among his harness bells and dust,
straight and even, slowly, as if each step
on that hard ground were precious.
He passes with a nod,
and stands at the door of his house,
making a final, brief inventory
all around and in it.

His wife goes in, comes out with a spoon,
hands it to you with a gracious little nod,
and says, "Such as . . ."

"Such as . . . ," as I heard
when my mother invited the preacher in,
or some old bum, who had fallen off
a box-car into our small town
and come looking for bread-crumbs,
a soup bowl of dish water beans,
a glass of tap water, served up
in a murky glass.
"Such as . . . ," as I heard
when I would walk across the tracks
into Bisbee, or Tucson, or El Paso, or Santa Fe,
bleeding behind the eyes,
cursing the slim-butted waitresses
who could be so polite.

"Such as . . . ," as I could even hear
in the girded ghettoes of New York.
"Such as . . . ," as I heard
when I was invited behind leaky doors,
into leaky rooms, for my loneliness,
for my hunger, for my blackness.
"Such as . . . ," as I hear
when people, who have only themselves to give,
offer you their meal.


## THE ALBUQUERQUE GRAVEYARD

It would be easier
to bury our dead
at the corner lot.
No need to wake
before sunrise,
take three buses,
walk two blocks,
search at the rear
of the cemetery,
to come upon the familiar names
with wilted flowers and patience.

But now I am here again.
After so many years
of coming here,
passing the sealed mausoleums,
the pretentious brooks and springs,
the white, sturdy limestone crosses,
the pattern of the place is clear to me.
I am going back
to the Black limbo,
an unwritten history
of our own tensions.
The dead lie here
in a hierarchy of small defeats.
I can almost see the leaders smile,
ashamed now of standing
at the head of those
who lie tangled
at the edge of the cemetery
still ready to curse and rage
as I do.
Here, I stop by the imitative cross
of one who stocked his parlor
with pictures of Robeson,
and would boom down the days,
dreaming of Othello's robes.
I say he never bothered me,
and forgive his frightened singing.
Here, I stop by the simple mound
of a woman who taught me
spelling on the sly,
parsing my tongue
to make me fit for her own dreams.
I could go on all day,
unhappily recognizing small heroes,
discontent with finding them here,
reproaches to my own failings.
Uneasy, I search the names
and simple mounds I call my own,
abruptly drop my wilted flowers,
and turn for home.

## LOVE IN THE WEATHER'S BELLS

Snow hurries
the strawberries
from the bush.
Star-wet water rides
you into summer,
into my autumn.
Your cactus hands
are at my heart again.
Lady, I court
my dream of you
in lilies and in rain.
I vest myself
in your oldest memory
and in my oldest need.
And in my passion
you are the deepest blue
of the oldest rose.
Star circle me an axe.
I cannot cut myself
from any of your emblems.
It will soon be cold here,
and dark here;
the grass will lie flat
to search for its spring head.
I will bow again
in the winter of your eyes.
If there is music,
it will be the weather's bells
to call me to the abandoned chapel
of your simple body.


## META-A AND THE A OF ABSOLUTES

I write my God in blue.
I run my gods upstream on flimsy rafts.
I bathe my goddesses in foam, in moonlight.
I take my reasons from my mother's snuff breath,
or from an old woman, sitting with a lemonade,
at twilight, on the desert's steps.

Brown by day and black by night,
my God has wings that open to no reason.
He scutters from the touch of old men's eyes,
scutters from the smell of wisdom, an orb
of light leaping from a fire.
Press him he bleeds.
When you take your hand to sacred water,
there is no sign of any wound.
And so I call him supreme, great artist,
judge of time, scholar of all living event,
the possible prophet of the possible event.
Blind men, on bourbon, with guitars,
blind men with their scars dulled by kola,
blind men seeking the shelter of a raindrop,
blind men in corn, blind men in steel,
reason by their lights that our tongues
are free, our tongues will redeem us.
Speech is the fact, and the fact is true.
What is moves, and what is moving is.
We cling to these contradictions.
We know we will become our contradictions,
our complex body's own desire.
Yet speech is not the limit of our vision.
The ear entices itself with any sound.
The skin will caress whatever tone
or temperament that rises or descends.
The bones will set themselves to a dance.
The blood will argue with a bird in flight.
The heart will scale the dew from an old chalice,
brush and thrill to an old bone.
And yet there is no sign to arrest us
                              from the possible.
We remain at rest there, in transit
from our knowing to our knowledge.
So I would set a limit where I meet my logic.
I would clamber from my own cave
into the curve of sign, an alphabet
of transformation, the clan's cloak of reason.
I am good when I am in motion,
when I think of myself at rest
in the knowledge of my moving,

when I have the vision of my mother at rest,
in moonlight, her lap the cradle of my father's head.
I am good when I trade my shells,
and walk from boundary to boundary,
unarmed and unafraid of another's speech.
I am good when I learn the world
through the touch of my present body.
I am good when I take the cove of a cub
                              into my care.
I am good when I hear the changes in my body
echo all my changes down the years,
when what I know indeed is what I would
                              know in deed.
I am good when I know the darkness of all light,
and accept the darkness, not as sign, but as my body.
This is the A of absolutes,
the logbook of judgments,
the good sign.


## THE LAKE IN CENTRAL PARK

It should have a woman's name,
something to tell us how the green skirt of land
                         has bound its hips.
When the day lowers its vermilion tapestry over the west ridge,
the water has the sound of leaves shaken in a sack,
and the child's voice that you have heard below
                              sings of the sea.

By slow movements of the earth's crust,
or is it that her hip bones have been shaped
by a fault of engineering?
Some coquetry cycles this blue edge,
a spring ready to come forth to correct
                         love's mathematics.

Saturday rises immaculately.
The water's jade edge plays against corn colored
picnic baskets, rose and lemon bottles, red balloons,
dancers in purple tights, a roan mare out of its field.
It is not the moment to think of Bahia
and the gray mother with her water explanation.
Not far from here, the city, a mass of swift water
in its own depression, licks its sores.

Still, I would be eased by reasons.
Sand dunes in drifts.
Lava cuts its own bed at a mountain base.
Blindness enters where the light refuses to go.
In Loch Lomond, the water flowers with algae
and a small life has taken the name of a star.

You will hear my star-slow heart
empty itself with a light-swift pitch
where the water thins to a silence.
And the woman who will not be named
screams in the birth of her fading away.


## MADRID

So the villa, having learned its many skills
through riding the bluish ochre waves of sand and clay,
has fooled us again. The moon is only a moon,
without the olive sheen and horse hoof of Granada.
No ruffled lace guitars clutch at the darkened windows.
The bilious green water marks on old houses
only make you think of the candle wind,
gathering its hammer force season after season,
a tempered master with a gray design.
Even the wall has been undone by sierra loneliness.

Perhaps on some theatrical night,
Lope fell in love with Elena,
and acted out her virtues,
until the father bored him.
That could only end in scandalous verses,

cuffs and a ticket out of Madrid,
a cloaked night at a village gate,
a loping horse and lovers shedding
                                    the acacia trees.
Better this picking at the poor brick and earth
than the bed where the mournful knight lies,
                            dreaming of dowry
               —some household furniture,
               an orchard, five vines, four beehives,
               forty-five hens, one cock and a crucible—
or the Italian guile and papal star of a duke's daughter.

It is late, and the voices of Tollán swing
on the porch of the Puerta de Alcalá.
Criollos dawdle in the Plaza Mayor,
brushing the white ruff of their provincial injuries.
The Panadería has gone, with its bull blood,
autos-da-fé and saints,
and the mimetic houses sink into shadow.
And yet that dead sun has awakened
the mountain mother in the oval plaza,
and these old women in black manta scudder
over the Manzares bed,
following the lights of Taxco silver, silk,
                    Luke's virgin and a good name.

It is late,
Palm Sunday,
on a day when the mask will drop
and a slouch hat and voluminous cloak
will uncover the exiled heart.
It is late,
the May day when the sun's red heart
                         returns from its exile,
and the Emperor's horsemen fall and begin
the unraveling of a Morning Star.
It is late,
when the Queen has gone,
in gentleman's attire,
to exhibit her hunger for boar meat
and a Bourbon husband with a taste for peace.

It is late,
when the red flag of the most violent summer
calls an end to the nation's yearning.

It is time
for the jeweled humiliation of the chosen
                 to be revealed.

Now when the snow falls on this crucible
of sullen winds and interrupted passions,
there will be the dark bell sound of a mother,
crying the name she can never have,
                 or having it, fulfill.


## DESIRE'S PERSISTENCE

> Yo ave del agua floreciente duro en fiesta.
> "Deseo de persistencia,"
> *Poesía Náhuatl*

1

In the region of rain and cloud,
I live in shade,
under·the moss mat of days bruised
                 purple with desire.
My dominion is a song in the wide ring of water.
There, I run to and fro,
braiding the logical act
          in the birth of an Ear of Corn,
polychromatic story I will now tell
in the weaving, power's form in motion,
a devotion to the unstressed.
Once, I wreathed around a king,
became a fishing-net, a maze,
          "a deadly wealth of robe."
Mothers who have heard me sing take heart;
I always prick them into power.

*Y vengo alzando al viento la roja flor*
*de invierno.*
I lift the red flower of winter into
the wind.
*Poesía Náhuatl*

I

Out of the ninth circle,
a Phoenician boat rocks upward into light
and the warmth of a name—given to heaven—
that arises in the ninth realm.
Earth's realm discloses the Egyptian
on the point of invention,
                deprived of life and death,
heart deep in the soul's hawk,
a thymos shadow knapping the tombed body.
Some one or thing is always heaven bound.
Some flowered log doubles my bones.
The spirit of Toltec turtledoves escapes.
A sharp, metaphorical cry sends me
                into the adorned sepulchre,
and the thing that decays learns
                how to speak its name.

Lift

Down Hidalgo,
past Alvarado and Basurto,
I walk a straight line
to the snailed Paseo Los Berros.
Here, at noon, the sun,
        a silver bead,
veils what the dawn has displayed.
Even so,
    I have taken up the morning's bond again
    —the lake with its pendulum leg
    shining in the distance,
    the boy in white
    hauling his bottle of chalky milk home.

I know I sit in the deep of a city
with its brocade of hills,
where a thin rain is an evening's fire.
I have heard the women sing
near their gas lamps,
when the rose end of day lights a hunger
for the garlanded soups and meat they prepare.
Often, I have taken the high ground
by the pond, over a frog's voice
            dampened by lilies,
and been exalted by the soothsayer
who knows I'm not at home.
I am the arcane body,
raised at the ninth hour,
to be welcomed by the moonlight
           of such spirited air.
I am the Dane of degrees
who realizes how the spirit glows
         even as it descends.

## Red

The heart, catalectic though it be, does glow,
responds to every midnight bell within you.
This is a discourse on reading heat,
the flushed char of burned moments one sees
after the sexton's lamp flows
over the body's dark book.
There is suspicion
here that violet
traces of
sacrifice
stand
bare.

## Flower

This marble dust recalls that sunset
with the best burgundy, and the way,
after the charm of it, the peacocks
escaped their cages on the green.
I would now embellish the flame
that ornaments you,
even as it once in that moment
            did.

I carry you blossomed,
cream and salt of a high crown.
You *must* flare,
            stream forth,
blister and scale me,
even as you structure the enveloping kiss,
                sporophore of our highest loss.


## Winter

Under the evergreens,
the grouse have gone under the snow.
Women who follow their fall flight
tell us that, if you listen, you can hear
their dove's voices ridge the air,
a singing that follows us to a bourne
                released from its heat sleep.
We have come to an imagined line,
                celestial,
that binds us to the burr of a sheltered thing
and rings us with a fire that will not dance,
                in a horn that will not sound.
We have learned, like these birds,
to publish our decline,
when over knotted apples and straw-crisp leaves,
the slanted sun welcomes us once again
to the arrested music in the earth's divided embrace.


## Wind

Through winter,
harmattan blacks the air.
My body fat with oil,
I become another star at noon,
when the vatic insistence
of the dog star's breath clings to me.
Though I am a woman,
I turn south,
toward the fire,
and hear the spirits in the bush.
But this is my conceit:
water will come from the west,
and I will have my trance,
                be reborn,

perhaps in a Mediterranean air,
the Rhone delta's contention
with the eastern side of rain.
In all these disguises,
I follow the aroma of power.
So I am charged in my own field,
to give birth to the solar wind,
particles spiraling around the line
                    of my body,
moving toward the disruption,
the moment when the oil of my star at noon
                              is a new dawn.

                                                    3

I shall go away, I shall disappear,
I shall be stretched on a bed of yellow roses
and the old women will cry for me.
So the Toltecas wrote: their books are finished,
but your heart has become perfect.


## THE WHITE DEER

The sun says she is there,
a dawn moon in a green field.

*I* imagine she came down,
riding the wooden horse ark;
or perhaps she was coiled within it,
and leapt from its serpent's embrace
when it lightly touched the earth.
But these are matters for a winter evening,
after the snow has been cleared,
and the thick docks of maple and birch
have been split and put away.
No need to resolve them now,
or to imagine that they are resolvable
without the enhanced water of the neighbors'
                    contemplation and resolve.

Before spring fully arrives,
we will all be thoroughly adept in her roots,
and able to hear her wet foot ripple the grass,
as she paddles from under the evergreens
                              into the clearing.

Night hunters seek her out.
I turn in the close air of my nightmares
because I hear their goose-voiced pickups
splash through the field's jade waves.
Those voices only serve to veil her.
                              And the light
the hunters cast in darkening circles
never seems to fix her white coat.

Deerjackers have the tail of things.
It would be better if they came,
              disarmed and in awe,
when she feeds on withering apples
                          and fallen buds,
when the only sound in a crowd of seekers
is a common breathing,
or the hushed tale of a memory like prayer.

I have grown,
day by day, in my own regard,
and in the distinction her tranquility
                          brings to the field.
I have grown, even though it is she
who has taken the field I say I own.

Each day I mark her pilgrim's satisfaction
and the way she satisfies these other pilgrims.

I would be taken into the depths of her crossed bones,
to encounter the seed that gave her such an exact light,
and to spiral under that clairvoyance that taught her to bear
                              her body with such grace.

Danger lies in that grace.
Danger lies in the moment when the others have come
to understand the seed's white presence, in a body
that could father us without a hint of solace,
and induce us to dance out of the first dream,
into betrayal, and the word that takes its first step
                                        into death.
Life here, I know, is a middle term,
breath arising from the arc and dimension
of a soul in wood, and the wood within a sheltered wood,
being a desert design, winding
            toward a new moon in a green field.

Night must fall upon your rosary of explanation.

Now, a man,
who has made himself intimate with the night,
sits, camouflaged, in a tree, and aims
his silent magnum at the white deer.


## COMPASSION'S BIRD

> I have been taught by dreams and fantasies.
> (Edwin Muir)

I know the incapacity of dream,
the failing copper light that falls upon
night's froggy skin, rises and flies, supreme,
above dawn's carapace, pale blue icon
of sleep and death, love's only eidolon.
Am I awakened by this firing pin,
a memory, bedizened by my twin?

I sleep again and know it false, a scheme
against the grain, the flashing circuit gone
awry; in that domain, I hear the scream
of elm, the pulsing hearts of angels on
a tear, the bold advance of bush, a wan-
ton thrust of force against my second skin,
and there in dream I lie, and lie therein.

We count the alphabet of fact extreme.
When all our measure sounds the carillon
of love's determined sphere, coordinates seem
to form the bone of myth, to lead head-on
to one intent of form, a going-on.
Now thát is góing, knowledge all akin
to grace, objective, sure, a Jacobin.

A braided water furs the bank. Mid-stream
I see a floating gold, the paragon
of loss, savannah twilight with its teem-
ing darkness still intact, my myrmidon.
I know there is that white phenomenon;
and up above the snowy shackles din
me home to this, the bliss of origin.

The book of sleep now opens to redeem
another valley, lost, and thereupon
abandoned, urging me through a gulf-stream
more apparent than fact, something quite spun
from that other memory not quite sun
enough to buckle me fast to the yin
and yang of love, not quite ecstasy's gin.

Oh, I should never think to blaspheme
against that mortality, be egged-on
into an inclining silence, cold-stream
given once and back to the Babylon
I abandoned for the sense of a gryphon,
inconsolable as death, not quite all in,
or all there, or sure of which way to spin.

And spin I do, tipped by cold self-esteem.
If I could write the tetragrammaton
of desire above my name, I would seem
to be free of hope, prolegomenon
to love's first betrayal, faith's hanger-on,
and set my own destruction. Within
love's discontent I recognize my twin.

Compassion's bird recedes; that is my theme
—resonant exile, a tempered agon.
No elastic universe can redeem
the pain of my heart's redshift, the python
embrace of madroños. I have gone
into the dense light of dream, origin
of love's structured star, love's own mandarin.

## DON JOSÉ GOROSTIZA
## ENCOUNTERS EL CORDOBÉS

> Victurosque dei celant ut vivere durent
> Felix esse mori.
> (From those who are to live the gods conceal
> The bliss of death; so they endure life.)
>
> Lucan, *Pharsalia*, IV, 519–520
> (tr. J. Wight Duff)

You wake in a Córdoba
disguised, bereft of its gold shoes and green
sash bound to its middle, yet you call it home,
or call it quaint, deceiving,
portent, prophecy, matron and, finally, Rome.
Here you can play with death, become a go-between,
a talent given to its own decay, sea-foam.

The heavy mango blooms and falls
greenly to rose
earth, where burrowing dogs come lately upon its
sweetness. Such wealth of intrusive calm befalls
us that night and coffee-fragrant air astound.
Would it be better to compose
the burning sugar cane, and water its sound?

José Gorostiza recalls
the lace repose
of a provincial Sunday, and hears in its rain
the slow course of a gypsy song that enthralls
him still, with the stillness of a page he found
in Lucan, ready to disclose
his own betrayal, senseless, himself spell-bound.

I remember going up
the Callejón Diamante, feeling unclean,
savoring the adobo and the palindrome
talk at the tables, the eyes
that seemed to promise adoration or the chrome
steel grip of the grave, nothing soft or as obscene
as envy, nothing set to the soul's metronome.

I will tell you what I hear.
Córdoba has a beggar's way with a song, a mean
gift for self-conscious display, a monochrome
alacrity for effect
—call it a clever youth, like you, Benedictine.
Still there is some virtue in its speech and, on the gnome-
like exactitude of its silence, a worthy sheen.

Such elegance stuns and appalls.
Time will expose
it for the crude burden it has become, a shield
against self-examination that forestalls
the same dispassionate crossing, the musclebound
spirit the spirit should oppose,
the shadow that rises, falls, goes underground.

A singer can adorn death's shawls,
and decompose
doubt's entangling fibre for the light in the cloth.
I hear they pay Annæus to build Chinese Walls
of sentiment, and raise from scratch a stamping-ground,
erect a Yanga to impose
upon our troubled dead and keep us safely bound.

I grudge thee thy death, José,
the stoic heart that faith allows me to demean.
How can I, gracefully, open the closed tome
of your suffering?      This voice
you hear is your own, spinning and turning the dome
of desire above us, set to endure, serene.
Annæus remembers death without end, rich loam.

# LUCILLE CLIFTON

## (B. 1936)

*At first glance, the poems of Lucille Clifton may appear slight, evanescent. This appearance, however, is deceiving, because these (usually) brief lyrics are capable, in an astonishing poetic sleight-of-hand, of plumbing the depths of personal and public experience and of rendering those depths with epigrammatic permanence. Ms. Clifton's poems are best heard aloud, where the words are articulated into voice, and the voice then summons the persona in a way that is uniquely her own, be it Lucille Clifton or one of the many identities she assumes and brings to light. Her poems can be read as a journal of black life since the mid-sixties (and before), and she has maintained a prolific level of high-quality production. Lucille Clifton was born in Depew, New York, and attended Howard University and Fredonia State Teachers College in New York. The author of poems, memoirs, and many children's books, she lives in Baltimore with her husband and family.*

### miss rosie

when i watch you
wrapped up like garbage
sitting, surrounded by the smell
of too old potato peels
or
when i watch you
in your old man's shoes
with the little toe cut out
sitting, waiting for your mind
like next week's grocery
i say
when i watch you
you wet brown bag of a woman
who used to be the best looking gal in georgia
used to be called the Georgia Rose
i stand up
through your destruction
i stand up

## the lost baby poem

the time i dropped your almost body down
down to meet the waters under the city
and run one with the sewage to the sea
what did i know about waters rushing back
what did i know about drowning
or being drowned

you would have been born into winter
in the year of the disconnected gas
and no car      we would have made the thin
walk over genesee hill into the canada wind
to watch you slip like ice into strangers' hands
you would have fallen naked as snow into winter
if you were here i could tell you these
and some other things

if i am ever less than a mountain
for your definite brothers and sisters
let the rivers pour over my head
let the sea take me for a spiller
of seas      let black men call me stranger
always      for your never named sake



light
on my mother's tongue
breaks through her soft
extravagant hip
into life.
lucille
she calls the light,
which was the name
of the grandmother
who waited by the crossroads
in virginia
and shot the whiteman off his horse,
killing the killer of sons.
light breaks from her life
to her lives . . .

mine already is
an afrikan name.

## cutting greens

curling them around
i hold their bodies in obscene embrace
thinking of everything but kinship.
collards and kale
strain against each strange other
away from my kissmaking hand and
the iron bedpot.
the pot is black,
the cutting board is black,
my hand,
and just for a minute
the greens roll black under the knife,
and the kitchen twists dark on its spine
and i taste in my natural appetite
the bond of live things everywhere.

driving through new england
by broken barns and pastures
i long for the rains of whydah
and the gardens
ripe as history
oranges and citron
limefruit and african apple
not just this springtime and
these wheatfields
white poets call the past.

the bodies broken on
the trail of tears
and the bodies melted
in middle passage
are married to rock and
ocean by now
and the mountains crumbling on
white men
the waters pulling white men down
sing for red dust and black clay
good news about the earth


## to ms. ann

i will have to forget
your face
when you watched me breaking
in the fields,
missing my children.

i will have to forget
your face
when you watched me carry
your husband's
stagnant water.

i will have to forget
your face
when you handed me
your house
to make a home,

and you never called me sister
then, you never called me sister
and it has only been forever and
i will have to forget your face.

## in salem

*to jeanette*

weird sister
the black witches know that
the terror is not in the moon
choreographing the dance of wereladies
and the terror is not in the broom
swinging around to the hum of cat music
nor the wild clock face grinning from the wall,
the terror is in the plain pink
at the window
and the hedges moral as fire
and the plain face of the white woman watching us
as she beats her ordinary bread.


## why some people be mad
## at me sometimes

they ask me to remember
but they want me to remember
their memories
and i keep on remembering
mine.


## 1.  at nagasaki

in their own order
the things of my world
glisten into ash. i
have done nothing
to deserve this,
only been to the silver birds
what they have made me.
nothing.

*them bones*
*them bones will*
*rise again*
*them bones*
*them bones will*
*walk again*
*them bones*
*them bones will*
*talk again*
*now hear*
*the word of The Lord*
            *—Traditional*

atlantic is a sea of bones,
my bones,
my elegant afrikans
connecting whydah and new york,
a bridge of ivory.

seabed they call it.
in its arms my early mothers sleep.
some women leapt with babies in their arms.
some women wept and threw the babies in.

maternal armies pace the atlantic floor.
i call my name into the roar of surf
and something awful answers.


**the death of crazy horse**
9/5/1877
age 35

in the hills where the hoop
of the world
bends to the four directions
WakanTanka has shown me
the path men walk is shadow.

i was a boy when i saw it,
that long hairs and grey beards
and myself
must enter the dream to be real.

so i dreamed and i dreamed
and i endured.

i am the final war chief.
never defeated in battle.
Lakotah, remember my name.

now on this walk my bones
and my heart
are warm in the hands of my father.
WakanTanka has shown me the shadows
will break
near the creek called Wounded Knee.

remember my name, Lakotah.
i am the final war chief.
father, my heart,
never defeated in battle,
father, my bones,
never defeated in battle,
leave them at Wounded Knee

and remember our name. Lakotah.
i am released from shadow.
my horse dreams and dances under me
as i enter the actual world.


## to my friend, jerina

listen,
when i found there was no safety
in my father's house
i knew there was none anywhere.
you are right about this,

how i nurtured my work
not my self, how i left the girl
wallowing in her own shame
and took on the flesh of my mother.
but listen,
the girl is rising in me,
not willing to be left to
the silent fingers in the dark,
and you are right,
she is asking for more than
most men are able to give,
but she means to have what she
has earned,
sweet sighs, safe houses,
hands she can trust.


## white lady
a street name for cocaine

wants my son
wants my niece
wants josie's daughter
holds them hard
and close as slavery
what will it cost
to keep our children
what will it cost
to buy them back.

white lady
says i want you
whispers
let me be your lover
whispers
run me through your
fingers
feel me smell me taste me
love me
nobody understands you like
white lady

white lady
you have chained our sons
in the basement
of the big house
white lady

you have walked our daughters
out into the streets
white lady
what do we have to pay
to repossess our children
white lady
what do we have to owe
to own our own at last


**powell   march 1991**

> "i am your worst nightmare"
> —black to white

this is that dream i wake from
crying, then clutch my sleeping wife
and rock her until i fall again
onto a battlefield. there,
they surround me, nations of darkness
speaking a language i cannot understand
and i suspect that something about
my life they know and hate and i hate them
for knowing it so well. my son,
i think about my son, my golden daughter,
and as they surround me, nearer, nearer,
i reach to pick up anything,
a tool, a stick, a weapon and
something begins to die. this
is that dream.

## 4/30/92
### for rodney king

so
the body
of one black man
is rag and stone
is mud
and blood
the body of one
black man
contains no life
worth loving
so the body
of one black man
is nobody
mama
mama
mamacita
is there no value
in this skin
mama
mama
if we are nothing
why
should we spare
the neighborhood
mama
mama
who will be next and
why should we save
the pictures

## slaveship

loaded like spoons
into the belly of Jesus
where we lay for weeks    for months
in the sweat and stink of our own
breathing
Jesus
why do you not protect us
chained to the heart of the Angel
where the prayers we never tell
are hot and red as our bloody ankles
Jesus
Angel
can these be men
who vomit us out from ships
called Jesus    Angel    Grace of God
onto a heathen country
Jesus
Angel
ever again
can this tongue speak
can this bone walk
Grace of God
can this sin live

jesus and angel and grace of god were the names of slaveships

■

# JAYNE CORTEZ
## (B. CA. 1936)

*Her Southwest origins in Arizona and California, as well as a deep
love for jazz and the blues, are integral to the poems of Jayne Cortez.
Her interests range from the aboriginal cultures of the United States
to the Spanish- and Portuguese-speaking diasporas of Latin and South
America to the very different groups of Africans in the New World.
These interests then overlap and intersect in a manner reminiscent of,
but quite different from, that of another southwestern native, Jay*

Wright. *The poems are narrated in a strong, storytelling voice that must be heard for full appreciation. Jayne Cortez is the author of seven books of poems and has made five recordings; she has been the recipient of two National Endowment for the Arts grants and sits on the Executive Board for the PEN American Center. She lives in New York City.*

## JAZZ FAN LOOKS BACK

I crisscrossed with Monk
Wailed with Bud
Counted every star with Stitt
Sang "Don't Blame Me" with Sarah
Wore a flower like Billie
Screamed in the range of Dinah
& scatted "How High The Moon" with Ella Fitzgerald
as she blew roof off the Shrine Auditorium
    Jazz at the Philharmonic

I cut my hair into a permanent tam
Made my feet rebellious metronomes
Embedded record needles in paint on paper
Talked bopology talk
Laughed in high pitched saxophone phrases
Became keeper of every Bird riff
every Lester lick
as Hawk melodicized my ear of infatuated tongues
& Blakey drummed militant messages in
soul of my applauding teeth
& Ray hit bass notes to the last love seat in my bones
I moved in triple time with Max
Grooved high with Diz
Perdidoed with Pettiford
Flew home with Hamp
Shuffled in Dexter's Deck
Squatty rooed with Peterson
Dreamed a "52nd Street Theme" with Fats
& scatted "Lady Be Good" with Ella Fitzgerald
as she blew roof off the Shrine Auditorium
    Jazz at the Philharmonic

## ADUPE

(ah doo pway)

1981 and
I did not find Nicolás Guillén
but I found Cuba
the Cuba in Nicolás Guillén's poetry
poetry dedicated to his two selves
his two sides
poetry in half notes
in eighth notes
in 6/8 time
poetry moving backward & forward like war dances
poetry doing the Rara in an African vocabulary
& I said
adupe   to Nicolás Guillén
Nicolás Banjo Guitar Mbira Guillén
improvising like the great instrument he is
in Yoruba
in Spanish
in Son
not exotic but Zydeco
not Miami but Havana
not tweet tweet but Mau Mau
adupe to the man from Camagüey

This morning
I went into the Paris of his poetry
& came out with poets clinking glasses to
nouveau beaujolais at Roquets
I pushed into favela of his poetry and
emerged with carnival costumes for
one hundred year celebration of the abolition of slavery
I looked through his blunt poetry and
saw exiles smiling like rusty bulldozers and acting
like disjointed chiefs of staff
like broken stags roaming in
everglades of khaki teeth & clandestine scrotum
I walked through seance house of his poetry and came upon
a fiesta sizzling in the bubble chamber of Aztec clouds

I dived into political content of his poetry and
discovered mysterious caves with odors of rotting
        imperialist dust
I looked at shell lined pelvis of his poetry and saw
infra-green heat of human capacity snaking down through
underground galaxy
of atomic clocks
I moved into stamina of his poetry and returned
with boxing gloves smelling like Santería shrines
I ran along the Malecón of his poetry and found
a poverty imbued with the power to drive straight through
a northern frente frio
I stood in stadium of his staccato yelping poetry and heard
messages coded and covered with drum heads from Oyo
and I said adupe Nicolás Guillén
adupe
for the cavalcade of leaves & moaning doves &
regalia of punching bags
adupe
for the musky cyclones in bolero jackets &
smoke filled consultation of yagruma trees
adupe
for the call & response of collaborating oceans &
the rooster juice splashed on feet steeped
in rumba motivations
adupe
for the great poem confrontations of Nicolás Guillén
adupe


Determination belongs to Guillén
Revolutionary thought belongs to Guillén
Solidarity belongs to Guillén
Gulla Efik Ewe Fula Fulani Twi belongs to Guillén
Mende Mandingo Mossi Umbundu Suk belongs to Guillén
Bomba la conga bomba belongs to Guillén
Negrismo Socialismo belongs to Guillén
Completeness of life in poetry belongs to Guillén
Nicolás Banjo Guitar Mbira Guillén
digging up roots and making his mark   making his mark
breaking those chains and making his mark   making his mark
mixing up rhythms and making his mark   making his mark

talking to his people and making his mark    making his mark
working with his work and making his mark    making his
    mark
Nicolás Banjo Guitar Mbira Guillén
Nicolás Banjo Guitar Mbira Guillén

*Adupe* means thanks in the Yoruba language spoken in Nigeria
*mbira*    African hand piano
*Mau Mau*    Kenyan revolutionary in colonial Kenya
*Gulla*    a Creolized English spoken in South Carolina
*Efik Ewe Fula Fulani Twi Mende Mandingo Mossi Umbundu Suk*
    African languages

■

# CLARENCE MAJOR

(B. 1936)

*Clarence Major is a wide-ranging and prolific author, working with
equal facility in poetry, fiction, and criticism. Unafraid of experimen-
tation, he has regularly pushed the boundaries of his work and ex-
plored many different techniques. "Swallow the Lake" is an example,
blending folk and modernist impulses into a great poem of the urban
dislocation faced by migrants to the city. Clarence Major was born in
Atlanta and grew up in Chicago. He attended the Art Institute of Chi-
cago and the University of Wisconsin, is the author of many books,
and is currently a professor of English at the University of California
at Davis.*

## SWALLOW THE LAKE

Gave me things I
could not use. Then. Now.
Rain night bursting upon & into. I
shine updown into Lake Michigan.

like the glow from the cold lights of the Loop.
Walks. Deaths. Births.
Streets. Things I could not give back. Nor
use. Or night or day or night or

loneliness. Other ways   feelings I could not
put into words   into themselves into people.
Blank monkeys of the hierarchy. More deaths—
stupidity & death turning them on

into the beat of my droopy heart   my middle
passage blues my corroding hate my release
while I come to become neon iron eyes stainless lungs
blood zincgripped steel I
come up abstract

not able to take their bricks. Tar. Nor their flesh.
I ran: stung. Loop fumes hung
                              in my smoky lungs.

ideas I could not break nor form. Gave me
things I
see break & run down the crawling down the
game.

Illusion illusion, and you
would swear before screaming somehow
choked voices in me.

The crawling thing in the blood, the
huge immune loneliness. One becomes immune
to the bricks the feelings. One becomes
death.
One becomes each one and every person I
become. I could not
I COULD NOT
I could not whistle and walk in storms
along Lake Michigan's shore. Concrete walks.
I could not swallow the lake

# ISHMAEL REED

## (B. 1938)

*The poems of Ishmael Reed are unlike any others being written by an American. Funny, often dark, simultaneously full of urbanity and mother wit, they are deceptively simple, combining complex reso-nances, deeply grounded history, and folk experience. Mr. Reed is a poet of the blues, in technique and content, and his poems are likely to surprise any reader who meets them with preconceived notions. Ishmael Reed was born in Chattanooga, Tennessee, and raised in Buf-falo, and he attended the State University of New York at Buffalo. He is the author of many books—fiction, poetry, essays—and has taught at Harvard, Yale, and Dartmouth. Currently, he teaches at the Uni-versity of California at Berkeley. He lives in Oakland.*

### I AM A COWBOY IN THE BOAT OF RA

'The devil must be forced to reveal any such
physical evil (potions, charms, fetishes, etc.) still
outside the body and these must be burned.'
(*Rituale Romanum*, published 1947, endorsed by
the coat-of-arms and introductory letter from
Francis cardinal Spellman)

I am a cowboy in the boat of Ra,
sidewinders in the saloons of fools
bit my forehead      like      O
the untrustworthiness of Egyptologists
who do not know their trips. Who was that
dog-faced man? they asked, the day I rode
from town.

School marms with halitosis cannot see
the Nefertiti fake chipped on the run by slick
germans, the hawk behind Sonny Rollins' head or
the ritual beard of his axe; a longhorn winding
its bells thru the Field of Reeds.

I am a cowboy in the boat of Ra. I bedded
down with Isis, Lady of the Boogaloo, dove
down deep in her horny, stuck up her Wells-Far-ago
in daring midday getaway. 'Start grabbing the
blue,' I said from top of my double crown.

I am a cowboy in the boat of Ra. Ezzard Charles
of the Chisholm Trail. Took up the bass but they
blew off my thumb. Alchemist in ringmanship but a
sucker for the right cross.

I am a cowboy in the boat of Ra. Vamoosed from
the temple i bide my time. The price on the wanted
poster was a-going down, outlaw alias copped my stance
and moody greenhorns were making me dance;
    while my mouth's
shooting iron got its chambers jammed.

I am a cowboy in the boat of Ra. Boning-up in
the ol West i bide my time. You should see
me pick off these tin cans whippersnappers. I
write the motown long plays for the comeback of
Osiris. Make them up when stars stare at sleeping
steer out here near the campfire. Women arrive
on the backs of goats and throw themselves on
my Bowie.

I am a cowboy in the boat of Ra. Lord of the lash,
the Loup Garou Kid. Half breed son of Pisces and
Aquarius. I hold the souls of men in my pot. I do
the dirty boogie with scorpions. I make the bulls
keep still and was the first swinger to grape the taste.

I am a cowboy in his boat. Pope Joan of the
Ptah Ra. C/mere a minute willya doll?
Be a good girl and
bring me my Buffalo horn of black powder
bring me my headdress of black feathers
bring me my bones of Ju-Ju snake
go get my eyelids of red paint.
Hand me my shadow

I'm going into town after Set

I am a cowboy in the boat of Ra

look out Set        here i come Set
to get Set          to sunset Set
to unseat Set       to Set down Set

                    usurper of the Royal couch
                    —imposter RAdio of Moses' bush
                    party pooper O hater of dance
                    vampire outlaw of the milky way


## DUALISM
In Ralph Ellison's *Invisible Man*

I am outside of
history. i wish
i had some peanuts, it
looks hungry there in
its cage

i am inside of
history. its
hungrier than i
thot


## PAUL LAURENCE DUNBAR IN
## THE TENDERLOIN

Even at 26, the hush when
you unexpectedly walked
into a theatre. One year
after *The History of Cakewalk.*

Desiring not to cause
a fuss, you sit alone
in the rear, watching a re
hearsal.
The actors are impressed. Wel
don Johnson, so super at des
cription, jots it all down.

I dont blame you for
disliking Whitman, Paul.
He lacked your style, like
your highcollared mandalaed
portrait in hayden's
*Kaleidoscope;* unobserved,
Death, the uncouth critic
does a first draft on your
            breath.


## .05

If i had a nickel
For all the women who've
Rejected me in my life
I would be the head of the
World Bank with a flunkie
To hold my derby as i
Prepared to fly chartered
Jet to sign a check
Giving India a new lease
On life

If i had a nickel for
All the women who've loved
Me in my life i would be
The World Bank's assistant
Janitor and wouldn't need
To wear a derby
All i'd think about would
Be going home

# THE REACTIONARY POET

If you are a revolutionary
Then I must be a reactionary
For if you stand for the future
I have no choice but to
Be with the past

Bring back suspenders!
Bring back Mom!
Homemade ice cream
Picnics in the park
Flagpole sitting
Straw hats
Rent parties
Corn liquor
The banjo
Georgia quilts
Krazy Kat
Restock

The syncopation of
Fletcher Henderson
The Kiplingesque lines
of James Weldon Johnson
Black Eagle
Mickey Mouse
The Bach Family
Sunday School
Even Mayor La Guardia
Who read the comics
Is more appealing than
Your version of
What Lies Ahead

In your world of
Tomorrow Humor
Will be locked up and
The key thrown away
The public address system
Will pound out headaches
All day
Everybody will wear the same
Funny caps
And the same funny jackets
Enchantment will be found
Expendable, charm, a
Luxury
Love and kisses
A crime against the state
Duke Ellington will be
Ordered to write more marches
"For the people," naturally

If you are what's coming
I must be what's going

Make it by steamboat
I likes to take it real slow


## NOV 22, 1988

In California
The day looks as though it's seen a ghost
An obstreperous storm is heading for the Sierras
The forecast is "cloudy gloomy and gray"
There is not a dry eye on TV,
They're showing the archival footage
Air Force One setting down in Dallas
the bouquet in Jackie's hands
the cruel scene in Washington as
politicians grapple with your coffin
the riderless horse,
little John John saluting
The face down in Cuba
Ich bin ein Berliner

You told the White Citizens
Councils that if you could
negotiate with Khrushchev then they could
negotiate with Negroes
You made old Miss
Swallow hard
You slammed Alabam'
stuffing its throat with
Jim Crow

Even on Dan Rather's face,
There is a struggle

It's been twenty years and
His youngest wants to know
Why did they murder you?
The theories are as common as homeless
People, huddled together in
The Port Authority
Under a bridge in Santa Cruz
Lafayette Park
Across the street from the White House
He agrees with the day
He feels like an old back pain
Eloisa wants to know, why
He is acting like a grinch
as he swivels, grumpily,
In her barber's chair
And maybe Carla is right when she says
You were like all the rest—only smoother
But when they took you out, Jack

it was as though
His generation was hit
In the belly with a medicine ball
They never fully recovered
Their wind
Their shape
Their tone and
They don't care what the
tabloids say, Jack
You are still their boy

And maybe it's best that you
left them, waving from a motorcade
A smile bigger than Texas
Fresh as that Oct. day Askia and He
saw you stride into the Carlyle Hotel
Bareheaded, unovercoated
Surrounded by men
Shaking in their long johns
It's not pretty what's become of US
It's like the room inside a grisly
Crime movie, about which the homicide
detective warns
"Don't go in there"
it smells like something
that's been dead in the sun
too long
It jerks about like the new chief's syntax

It has the style of an inside
trader's ill-fitting collar
It bungles along like
your lunkish successors
in black tie, and tails, executing a mean
Fox Trot at the Inaugural
Ball

# MICHAEL S. HARPER

## (B. 1938)

*Michael Harper credits his abruptly altered adolescence—moving
with his family from Brooklyn to Los Angeles at the age of thir-
teen—with awakening his poetic sensibility, tuning him in to the ex-
traordinary differences in American society, and encouraging his
curiosity about the depths and nuances of those differences. Mr. Har-
per is often described as a poet of jazz and the blues; this label, in his
case, is ultimately reductionist. He is, first and last, a poet of history,
and of America, and the musical references are but one tool, or color,*

*that he uses in his explorations of what has happened—to black and white and most of the others—on this continent. Influenced by Frost, Roethke, Yeats, Hayden, Hughes, and Auden, Mr. Harper probes the things that link Americans, and has a special gift for probing the pain that results when those links are sundered. Michael Harper was educated at California State University at Los Angeles and the University of Iowa, and is at present University Professor at Brown University. He lives with his family in Providence, Rhode Island.*

## FOR BUD

Could it be, Bud
that in slow galvanized
fingers beauty seeped
into *bop* like Bird
*weed* and Diz clowned—
Sugar waltzing
back into dynamite,
sweetest left hook you
ever dug, baby;
could it violate violence
Bud, like Leadbelly's
chaingang chuckle,
the candied yam
twelve string clutch
of all blues:
there's no rain
anywhere, soft
enough for you.

## REMEMBER MEXICO

Villages of high quality
merchandise—hand-tooled leather,
blown glass like diamonds,
cloth finer than linen,
delicious food without dysentery,

mountain water from palapa groves
cured by glistening rocks,
burro-drawn carts for the day,
fishing boats destined for clear
water and giant marlin;
the peasants clean
tanned and bilingual;
lemon, papaya,
horseback or raft,
turtle in the picnic
baskets, white lunch
on hacienda siesta—
pure and unblemished
in the public notices.

I remember the birds
of the desert
ripping a horse
not yet fallen;
hookworm, beetles,
the soup of the desert;
cows and donkeys
eat around the cracked
and broken American
automobiles; in this covey
of linkage, spoken here,
I think of Montezuma's
unspeakable rites
in honed rock graves—
bloodmeal and black tunnels;
Indians who speak no Spanish
and worship the sea,
fruit unpicked in suspect
sweetness for corn,
diesel smoke forcing
Indian, and Indian
and Indian, and Indian
farther up the mountainside.

## AMERICAN HISTORY

Those four black girls blown up
in that Alabama church
remind me of five hundred
middle passage blacks,
in a net, under water
in Charleston harbor
so *redcoats* wouldn't find them.
Can't find what you can't see
can you?


## HERE WHERE COLTRANE IS

Soul and race
are private dominions,
memories and modal
songs, a tenor blossoming,
which would paint suffering
a clear color but is not in
this Victorian house
without oil in zero degree
weather and a forty-mile-an-hour wind;
it is all a well-knit family:
*a love supreme.*
Oak leaves pile up on walkway
and steps, catholic as apples
in a special mist of clear white
children who love my children.
I play "Alabama"
on a warped record player
skipping the scratches
on your faces over the fibrous
conical hairs of plastic
under the wooden floors.

Dreaming on a train from New York
to Philly, you hand out six
notes which become an anthem
to our memories of you:

oak, birch, maple,
apple, cocoa, rubber.
For this reason Martin is dead;
for this reason Malcolm is dead;
for this reason Coltrane is dead;
in the eyes of my first son are the browns
of these men and their music.


## LAST AFFAIR: BESSIE'S BLUES SONG

Disarticulated
arm torn out,
large veins cross
her shoulder intact,
her tourniquet
her blood in ail-white big bands:

*Can't you see*
*what love and heartache's done to me*
*I'm not the same as I used to be*
*this is my last affair*

Mail truck or parked car
in the fast lane,
afloat at forty-three
on a Mississippi road,
Two-hundred-pound muscle on her ham bone,
'nother nigger dead 'fore noon:

*Can't you see*
*what love and heartache's done to me*
*I'm not the same as I used to be*
*this is my last affair*

Fifty-dollar record
cut the vein in her neck,
fool about her money
toll her black train wreck,
white press missed her fun'ral
in the same stacked deck:

*Can't you see*
*what love and heartache's done to me*
*I'm not the same as I used to be*
*this is my last affair*

Loved a little blackbird
heard she could sing,
Martha in her vineyard
pestle in her spring,
Bessie had a bad mouth
made my chimes ring:

*Can't you see*
*what love and heartache's done to me*
*I'm not the same as I used to be*
*this is my last affair*


## HOMAGE TO THE NEW WORLD

Surrounded by scientists in a faculty
house, the trees wet with hot rain,
grass thickening under the trees,
welcomers come, ones and twos,
gifts of shoehorns, soap, combs,
half a subscription to the courier,
some news about changing
plates, the nearest market,
how to pick up the trash, a gallon
of milk twice a week, OK?

On the third day here,
a friend came in the night to announce
a phone call and a message,
and heard the shell go in
and the rifle cocking,
our next-door animal-vet neighbor,
and cried out, "Don't shoot,"
and walked away to remember the phone
and the message, the crickets,
and the rifle cocking,
grass and hot rain.

I write in the night air
of the music of Coltrane,
the disc of his voice in this
contralto heart, my wife;
*so what! Kind of Blue,*
these fatherless whites
come to consciousness
with a history of the gun—
the New World, if misery had
a voice, would be a rifle cocking.

## NIGHTMARE BEGINS RESPONSIBILITY

I place these numbed wrists to the pane
watching white uniforms whisk over
him in the tube-kept
prison
fear what they will do in experiment
watch my gloved stickshifting gasolined hands
breathe *boxcar-information-please* infirmary tubes
distrusting white-pink mending paperthin
silkened end hairs, distrusting tubes
shrunk in his *trunk-skincapped*
shaven head, in thighs
*distrusting-white-hands-picking-baboon-light*
on this son who will not make his second night
of this wardstrewn intensive airpocket
where his father's asthmatic
hymns of *night-train*, train done gone
his mother can only know that he has flown
up into essential calm unseen corridor
going boxscarred home, *mamaborn, sweetsonchild*
*gonedowntown* into *researchtestingwarehousebatteryacid*
*mama-son-done-gone*/me telling her 'nother
train tonight, no music, no breathstroked
heartbeat in my infinite distrust of them:

and of my distrusting self
*white-doctor-who-breathed-for-him-all-night*
say it for two sons gone,
say nightmare, say it loud
panebreaking heartmadness:
nightmare begins responsibility.


## GRANDFATHER

In 1915 my grandfather's
neighbors surrounded his house
near the dayline he ran
on the Hudson
in Catskill, NY
and thought they'd burn
his family out
in a movie they'd just seen
and be rid of his kind:
the death of a lone black
family is *the Birth
of a Nation*,
or so they thought.
His 5'4" waiter gait
quenched the white jacket smile
he'd brought back from watered
polish of my father
on the turning seats,
and he asked his neighbors
up on his thatched porch
for the first blossom of fire
that would burn him down.

They went away, his nation,
spittooning their torched necks
in the shadows of the riverboat
they'd seen, posse decomposing;
and I see him on Sutter
with white bag from your
restaurant, challenged by his first
grandson to a foot-race
he will win in white clothes.

I see him as he buys galoshes
for his railed yard near Mineo's
metal shop, where roses jump
as the el circles his house
toward Brooklyn, where his rain fell;
and I see cigar smoke in his eyes,
chocolate Madison Square Garden chews
he breaks on his set teeth,
stitched up after cancer,
the great white nation immovable
as his weight wilts
and he is on a porch
that won't hold my arms,
or the legs of the race run
forwards, or the film
played backwards on his grandson's eyes.


## TONGUE-TIED IN BLACK AND WHITE

—"I had a most marvelous piece of luck. I died."

In Los Angeles
while the mountains cleared of smog
your songs dreamed
Jefferson and Madison
walking hand in hand
as my grandfather walked to Canada.
What eyes met the black student
next to me, her hands fanning
your breezy neck from this veranda,
but Henry's/Mr. Bones.

Home from Mexico and you in LIFE,
I walk dead center into the image
of LBJ cloistered by the draping
flags of Texas and the confederacy,
and as my aunt of Oklahoma told me
I understand your father's impulse
to force you into Crane's nightmare.

After the Roethke reading in Seattle
you stroked the stout legs of an ex-
student's wife while he sketched
you in adoration and as you cautioned
your audience, "45 minutes and no longer,"
how Harvard paid in prestige not money,
how a man at Harvard read for four hours,
that he ought to be set down in the Roman
courtyard and have rocks set upon him
until death—your audience laughed.

You admired my second living son
as you loved the honeyed dugs of his mother,
your spotless tan suit weaving in the arch
where goalposts supported you in foyer
for you would not fall.

At your last public reading,
let out for fear of incident without a drink,
your foot bandaged from fire you'd
stamped out in a wastebasket of songs,
your solitary voice speckled in Donne,
in Vermont where the stories of Bread
Loaf, Brown, another broken leg abandoned
in monotones of your friends studying you;

Now I must take up our quarrel:
never dangerous with women
though touched by their nectared hair;
you wrote in that needful black idiom
offending me, for only your inner voices
spoke such tongues, your father's soft prayers
in an all black town in Oklahoma; your ear lied.
*That slave in you was white blood forced to derision,*
those seventeenth-century songs saved you from
      review.

Naked, in a bottle of Wild Turkey,
the bridge you dived over was your source:
St. Paul to St. Louis to New Orleans,
the *asiento*, Toussaint, border ruffians,
signature of Lincoln, porters bringing
messages to white widows of Europe,

a classics major, and black, taking your classes,
the roughpage of your bird legs and beard
sanitizing your hospital room,
the last image of your bandaged foot
stamping at flames on the newborn bridge.

This is less than the whole truth
but it is the blacker story
and what you asked to be told:
"lay off the sauce when you write"
you said to me, winking at the brownskinned
actress accompanying me to the lectern;
and how far is Texas from Canada
and our shared relatives in blacktown
on the outskirts of your tongue, tied still.


## EVE (RACHEL)

> "What has gone into that quality of voice, that
> distancing, that precise knowledge of who she is,
> where she has come from, what costs have been to
> herself, but also to others, the ones who did not
> survive."

> "the rib is but the unseen potential aspect of self,
> free of fleshly desire, waiting to be discovered, to be
> named beyond definition, a conjugation of names in
> deeds."

I have been waiting to speak to you
for many years; one evening
I sat down to tell the story
of your mother's song of *Fante*,
"The Dance of the Elephants"
on the lips of her parents
escaping in disguise.
From this ribbed podium I have waited
for you to join my own daughter,
Rachel, in the arena of surrender,
where women bathe the wounds
in our dark human struggle to be human:
*this must be earned in deeds.*

There are blessings to remember:
your magical birth on the third
anniversary of your parents' wedding.
I was there among the family faces
strung on violin and cello,
your Irish grandmother's song of the bogs,
your hidden grandfather's raging at your loveliness,
at his own daughters swimming amidst swans.

I talk of you to your parents over these distancings,
our voices rising over gray Portland skies,
the lush green of your eyes
shuttered in springtime;
you can not be otherwise than your grandmothers'
healing songs sprouting through you,
a tree in essential bloom in standing water.

To be here in America?
Ask this of the word many times:
in your parents' books underlined in green,
in dark blotches of your live-giving womb,
in these riddles beckoning—
"old folk songs chanted underneath the stars,"
in the cadence of black speech:
"just like a tree; backwater, muddy water,"
in gentle eyes of these writers of kinship,
in the circle of light which is Little Crow,
skinned and diced folksaying his splintered story,
comforts in small utterances, remember,
Eve means rescue from bodily desire.

Our last welcome
is the love of liars
in tall tales to larger truths;
succor these voices in your blood
listening for doubletalk, stoicism, irony
where your heart-center funnels its loam,
where you will plant your own crafted shoes
in these bodies of soiled, broken, mending hands.

## DOUBLE ELEGY

Whatever city or country road
you two are on
there are nettles,
and the dark invisible
elements cling to your skin
though you do not cry
and you do not scratch
your arms at forty-five degree angles
as the landing point of a swan
in the Ohio, the Detroit River;

at the Paradise Theatre
you named the cellist
with the fanatical fingers
of the plumber, the exorcist,
and though the gimmickry at wrist
and kneecaps could lift the séance
table, your voice was real
in the gait and laughter of Uncle
Henry, who could dance on either
leg, wooden or real, to the sound
of the troop train, megaphone,
catching the fine pitch of a singer
on the athletic fields of Virginia.

At the Radisson Hotel,
we once took a fine angel
of the law to the convention center,
and put her down as an egret
in the subzero platform of a friend—
this is Minneapolis, the movies
are all of strangers, holding themselves
in the delicacy of treading water,
while they wait for the trumpet
of the 20th Century Limited
over the bluff or cranny.
You two men like to confront
the craters of history and spillage,
our natural infections of you
inoculating blankets and fur,
ethos of cadaver and sunflower.

I hold the dogwood blossom,
eat the pear, and watch the nettle
swim up in the pools
of the completed song
of Leadbelly and Little Crow
crooning the buffalo and horse
to the changes and the bridge
of a twelve-string guitar,
the melody of "Irene";
this is really goodbye—
I can see the precious stones
of embolism and consumption
on the platinum wires of the mouth:
in the flowing rivers, in the public baths
of Ohio and Michigan.

## IN HAYDEN'S COLLAGE

Van Gogh would paint the landscape
green—or somber blue;
if you could see the weather
in Amsterdam in June, or August,
you'd cut your lobe too,
perhaps simply on heroin,
the best high in the world,
instead of the genius of sunflowers,
blossoming trees. The Japanese
bridge in Hiroshima,
precursor to the real impression,
modern life, goes to Windsor, Ontario,
or Jordan, or the Natchez
Trace. From this angle, earless,
a torsioned Django Rhinehart
accompanies Josephine. You know
those rainbow children couldn't
get along in this *ole worl'*.

Not over that troubled water;
and when the band would play once
too often in Arkansas, or Paris,
you'd cry because the sunset was too
bright to see the true colors,
the first hue, and so nearsighted
you had to touch the spiderman's
bouquet; you put your arcane colors
to the spatula and cook
to force the palate in the lion's
den—to find God in all the light
the paintbrush would let in—
the proper colors,
the corn, the wheat, the valley,
dike, the shadows, and the heart
of self—minnow of the universe,
your flaccid fishing pole,
pieced together, never broken, never end.


## THE DROWNING OF THE FACTS
## OF A LIFE

Who knows why we talk of death
this evening, warm beyond the measure
of breath; it will be cool tomorrow
for in the waters off Long Beach
my brother's ashes still collect
the flowers of my mother and father,
my sister dropped in the vase
of a face they made of old places,
the text of water.

Tonight we talk of losses in the word
and go on drowning in acts of faith
knowing so little of humility,
less of the body,
which will die in the mouth of reality.

This foolish talk in a country
that cannot pronounce napalm
or find a path to a pool of irises
or the head of a rose.

My brother was such a flower;
he would spring into my path
on a subway train, above the ground
now, on the way home from school,
letting the swift doors pinch
his fingers of books and records,
house supplies from the corner market,
as he leaped back to the station
platform, crying his pleasure
to his brother,
who was on the train . . .
getting off at next exit
to look for him.

This is how we make our way home:
Each day when the Amtrak express
on the northeast corridor
takes my heritage from Boston
to the everglades of Maryland,
I think of the boy who sat
on the platform in the Canarsie,
on the uneven projects of New Lots
Avenue, BMT:

he was so small he could slip
through the swinging chains
of the express train
on the Williamsburg Bridge,
and not get touched by the third rail,
the chain link fencing of the accordion
swiveling to the swing and curses
of the motorman.

A fortnight my brother lay in coma,
his broken pate and helmet
in a shopping bag of effects,
his torn-off clothes and spattering
coins, the keys to the golden Yamaha—
with remnants of pavement in his scalp,
the trace of jacket laid under his head,
the black Continental idling
at anchor with the infinite,
the same black ice of the subway.

I came to chant over his fungus-
eaten flesh, allergic to his own
sweat, sweeter than the women
and children collecting
in caravan behind him; the Oriental
nurses, so trained in the cadence
of thermometer and brain scan,
came in their green bracelets
and uniforms to relieve him—

a catheter of extract
makes the pomade of his hair
disappear, for his lips twitch
in remembrance at impact,
rage at the power of love,
the welcome table and tabernacle
for his broken shoes and helmet.

Ponder the spent name of Jonathan,
apple and brother in the next
world, where the sacred text
of survival is buried in the bosom
of a child, radiated
in moonlight forever.
I touch the clean nostril
of the body in his mechanical
breathing, no chant sound enough
to lift him from the rest
of contraption
to the syncopated dance of his name.

# THE LOON

The estate bird
sits on the water
outside my window;
if you watch long
enough you will see
her dive
from her canopy,
and in the understory
of the weather,
in trees,
beneath the surface,
you might see another
estate bird.

In this scene the call
goes out to the ground cover,
where you can lay your face,
unbroken by the ceremonial
tears of the funeral,
on ferns.

Oh deciduous pouch
of awful leaves
at a would-be cemetery,
listen to the loon.

You could dream conifers,
the deep roots of burrowing
animals and insects,
the opossum
drunk on his tail
hearing the interior voice
of secret soil layer
where we bury her.

# STUDS

                    the cut, a cut above a star,
                    rested in the womb and hands—

Off-color eyes that shine through lobes,
the flesh still uneaten by stickpin,
he was stuck to her; this attachment,
like string from the loops of i.u.d.
caught him unawares, in planes
above the earth, on plains
near the homestead, on water
which he has touched with his belt
and bow, as a lifeguard,
before he met her.
                    Yes, she could brown
in that sun, the broad shoulders
concealed in flesh for his children,
who grew beyond her; he built a shed
for her tools, the garden, the chain-saw—
windows faced toward the southern estuary
where turtles called, for the pond
swelled in the porous ground,
from springs, and she was a spring.

All day he has thought of Seminoles;
all day he has dreamed of the Narragansett;
his children could fit in if the drum
were opened to shells he could use
for the dinner table, and shells
from the sea decorate the walls
of the uterus, mystery of caves
he got lost in on special dates,
January 15 for instance,
now a national holiday;
and April 23, her father's birthday,
and Shakespeare's,
where he read in a long line
at the Library of Congress
after visiting the Capitol
where Martin Luther King, Jr.
stood in consummate black stone.

Now he must ask about diamonds;
how refraction turns into bloodlines
he could choose for band music,
the territory bands
of Count Basie, without charts,
in a beat-up van,
passing for Indians,
passing in the slow lane
through the culture.

He would place her flesh there;
he would ask her to wear these,
diamond studs, in each ear,
to hear his song: to hear his name
come alive in her ears.

*for Shirley*

■

# AL YOUNG

## (B. 1939)

*Al Young has, in his poetry, married the lush romanticism of the nine-*
*teenth century to the dark sonorities of jazz and the blues, forming, at*
*their best, poems that are tender, melancholy, and purely American.*
*Mr. Young is interested in a great many things: music, dance, love (pla-*
*tonic, romantic, and family), contemporary history, the journey of the*
*man known as "Al Young" from his beginnings as a black child in*
*rural Mississippi to his present status as a mature world traveler.*
*These and other subjects find their way into his work, and are felt,*
*imagined, and described with an honesty that can be original and*
*startling. Al Young was born in Ocean Springs, Mississippi, and was*
*educated at the University of Michigan. He is the author of more than*
*ten books, including poetry, novels, and memoirs, and has edited,*
*with Ishmael Reed, two anthologies of poetry. He has taught at Stan-*
*ford and Rice universities, the University of California at Berkeley,*
*and the University of Washington. He currently lives in Palo Alto,*
*California.*

# DANCE OF THE INFIDELS

*in memory of Bud Powell*

The smooth smell of Manhattan taxis,
Parisian taxis, it doesnt matter, it's
the feeling that modern man is all youve
laid him out to be in those tinglings & rushes;
the simple touch of your ringed fingers
against a functioning piano.

                         The winds of Brooklyn
still mean a lot to me. The way certain chicks
formed themselves & their whole lives around
a few notes, an attitude more than anything.
I know about the being out of touch, bumming
nickels & dimes worth of this & that off
him & her here & there—everything but
hither & yon.

            Genius does not grow on trees.

                                I owe
you a million love dollars & so much more than
thank-you for re-writing the touch & taste & smell
of the world for me those city years when I could
very well have fasted on into oblivion.

                            Ive just
been playing the record you made in Paris with Art
Blakey & Lee Morgan. The european audience
is applauding madly. I think of what Ive heard
of Buttercup's flowering on the Left Bank & days
you had no one to speak to. Wayne Shorter is
beautifying the background of sunlight with
children playing in it & shiny convertibles
& sedans parked along the blocks as I blow.

                            Grass
grows. Negroes. Women walk. The world, in case
youre losing touch again, keeps wanting the same
old thing.

You gave me some of it; beauty I sought
before I was even aware how much I needed it.

                                    I know
this world is terrible & that one must, above all,
hold onto the heart & the hearts of others.

                          I love *you*


## DETROIT 1958

Only parts of the pain of living
may be captured in a poem or
tale or song or in the image seen.

Even in life we only halfway feel
the tears of a brother or sister,
mass disenchantment in cities,
our discovery of love's meagerness,
the slow rise and fall of the sun.

Sadness is the theme of existence;
joy its variations. Pain is only a portion
of sadness, and efforts to escape it
can lead to self-destruction,
one aspect of pain lived imaginatively.

It is in life that we celebrate pain;
It is an art that we imitate it.

Beauty is saddening, or, as the man sings,
"The bitter note makes the song so sweet."

# HOW THE RAINBOW WORKS

*for Jean Cook, on learning of her*
*mother's death*

Mostly we occupy ocular zones, clinging
only to what we think we can see.
We can't see wind or waves of thought,
electrical fields or atoms dancing;
only what they do or make us believe.

Look on all of life as color—
vibratile movement, heart-centered,
from invisibility to the merely visible.
Never mind what happens when one of us dies.
Where are you before you even get born?
Where am I and all the unseeable souls
we love at this moment, or loathed
before birth? Where are we right now?

Everything that ever happened either
never did or always will with variations.
Let's put it another way: Nothing ever
happened that wasn't dreamed, that wasn't
sketched from the start with artful surprises.
Think of the dreamer as God, a painter,
a ham, to be sure, but a divine old master
whose medium is light and who sidesteps
tedium by leaving room both inside and outside
this picture for subjects and scenery to wing it.

Look on death as living color too: the dyeing
of fabric, submersion into a temporary sea,
a spectruming beyond the reach of sensual
range which, like time, is chained to change;
the strange notion that everything we've
ever done or been up until now is past
history, is gone away, is bleached, bereft,
perfect, leaving the scene clean to freshen
with pigment and space and leftover light.

## LESTER LEAPS IN

Nobody but Lester let Lester leap
into a spotlight that got too hot
for him to handle, much less keep
under control like thirst in a drought.

He had his sensitive side, he had
his hat, that glamorous porkpie whose
sweatband soaked up all that bad
leftover energy.

          How did he choose
those winning titles he'd lay on favorites
—Sweets Edison, Sir Charles, Lady Day?
Oooo and his sound! Once you savor its
flaming smooth aftertaste, what do you say?

Here lived a man so hard and softspoken
he had to be cool enough to hold his horn
at angles as sharp as he was heartbroken
in order to blow what it's like being born.


## THE BLUES DON'T CHANGE

> "Now I'll tell you about the
> Blues. All Negroes like Blues.
> Why? Because they was born with
> the Blues. And now everybody
> have the Blues. Sometimes they
> don't know what it is."
>
>         —Leadbelly

And I was born with you, wasn't I, Blues?
Wombed with you, wounded, reared and forwarded
from address to address, stamped, stomped
and returned to sender by nobody else but you,
Blue Rider, writing me off every chance you
got, you mean old grudgeful-hearted, table-
turning demon, you, you sexy soul-sucking gem.

Blue diamond in the rough, you *are* forever.
You can't be outfoxed don't care how they cut
and smuggle and shine you on, you're like a
shadow, too dumb and stubborn and necessary
to let them turn you into what you ain't
with color or theory or powder or paint.

That's how you can stay in style without sticking
and not getting stuck. You know how to sting
where I can't scratch, and you move from frying
pan to skillet the same way you move people
to go to wiggling their bodies, juggling their
limbs, loosening that goose, upping their voices,
opening their pores, rolling their hips and lips.

They can shake their bodies but they can't shake *you.*


## HOW STARS START

I don't ask to be forgiven
nor do I wish to be given up,
not entirely, not yet, not while
pain is shooting clean through
the only world I know: this one.
There is no Mal Waldron song or
Marlene Dietrich epic in black
& white where to scrawl against
the paradigms of time is to mean
something benign, like dismissing
present actions or behavior because
I know & understand deep down
inside & beyond that life itself
is acting all of this out; this ˜
kamikaze drama, cosmic if you
will, but certainly comic, in a style
so common as to invite confusion.

Who am I now? What have I become?
Where do we draw the line between being
who I am and what I ought to be?
Need is a needle, nosing its sticky load
into my grief, spilling into veins
that can't be sewn, transforming their dark
cells into lighted semblances of relief.
The stomach is involved; flesh itself;
memories of an island doom that leaves
no room for sense or sensitive
assessments of truth about myself.
Which is the me that never changes?

All roads lead back to starts, to where
I started out, to stars: the fiery
beginnings of our ends & means; our
meanness & our meanings. There never
was a night begun in darkness,
nor a single day begun in light.


## JAZZ AS WAS

Sometimes it's the flagrant accentuation
of bebop & late afternoon loneliness
that devastates; those early night
hours just don't get it, so everything
that happens long past midnight grows
misty with whiskey & other forms
of practiced behavior. The drummer's
got some new white girl on hold who adores him.
The piano player's totally clean but
won't comb her hair; she's hip to the bone.
The bassist is a communist the way
he scribbles off accompaniment like a giant
bear waltzing africally thru bureaucratic
steps. Hey, it's America heard in rhythm
& enormous harmonies the color of October;
swollen & falling, full of seedy surprises
that make your hoary heart speed up
& do double time between the born-again beats.

## FROM BOWLING GREEN

The prompt sadness of Schumann or Tchaikovsky
is the wistfulness of Basho or Bukowski
in a furnished apartment that happens
to hold me now in January-glacial splendor.
As love condenses into ice and snow
forms the steam that bleeds from molten lava,
so music and its poetry will ooze
with sweet symphonic arias and blues.
Getting used to appearing in a poem or song
means becoming comfortable with life. The long
way around usually ends up being the shortcut.


## LEAVING SYRACUSE

All these girls licking & sucking
their own twitchy fingers free of chocolate
were winos once on well-policed benches,
or smoking in urine-lined johns.

The lyrical light of Greyhound,
its bright snowiness the color of Rip
Van Winkle's beard, erect with winter,
lushes up the loveliest of valleys.
Those trucks & barns & frozen

slopes as up-and-down as chimney smoke
give you plenty to shine on.

Joy is with us all the time
we're being bused from one universe
to the next. Dappled or evenly iced over,
these subtle imitations of life keep
on the move. Good morning, Rochester,
have you heard the news?

# HAKI MADHUBUTI

## (B. 1942)

*The poems of Haki Madhubuti are by turns comic, tragic, tender, en-*
*raged, and melancholic, sometimes all at once, as they narrate the*
*events and emotions of times of tremendous turmoil in America. Mr.*
*Madhubuti's poems are honest and probing, and are often as hard, or*
*harder, on blacks as on whites in their social criticisms. Mr. Madhu-*
*buti, born Don L. Lee in Little Rock, moved to Chicago as a teenager*
*and attended high school and college there. He has taught at Roose-*
*velt, Cornell, and Northeastern Illinois universities and the Univer-*
*sity of Illinois at Chicago. He has published many volumes of poetry,*
*as well as essays and criticism, and in the last several years has been*
*extremely involved in working with black youngsters and youths on*
*the South Side of Chicago.*


## THE SELF-HATRED OF DON L. LEE
(9/22/63)

i,
at one time,
loved
my
color—
it
opened sMALL
doors of
tokenism
&
acceptance.
  (doors called, "the only one" & "our negro" )
after painfully
struggling
thru Du Bois,

Rogers, Locke
Wright & others,
my blindness
was vanquished
by pitchblack
paragraphs of
"us, we, me, i"
awareness.

i
began
to love
only a
part of
me—
my inner
self which
is all
black—
&
developed a
vehement
hatred of
my light
brown
outer.


## GWENDOLYN BROOKS

she doesn't wear
costume jewelry
& she knew that walt disney
was/is making a fortune off
false-eyelashes and that time magazine is the
authority on the knee/grow.
her makeup is total-real.

a negro english instructor called her:
    "a fine negro poet."
a whi-te critic said:
    "she's a credit to the negro race."
somebody else called her:
    "a pure negro writer."
johnnie mae, who's a senior in high school said:
    "she & langston are the only negro poets we've
    read in school and i understand her."
pee wee used to carry one of her poems around in his back pocket;
    the one about being cool. that was befo pee wee
    was cooled by a cop's warning shot.

into the sixties
a word was born . . . . . . . . BLACK
& with black came poets
& from the poet's ball points came:
black doubleblack purpleblack blueblack beenblack was
black daybeforeyesterday blackerthan ultrablack super
black blackblack yellowblack niggerblack blackwhi-teman
blackerthanyoueverbes 1/4 black unblack coldblack clear
black my momma's blackerthanyourmomma pimpleblack fall
black so black we can't even see you black on black in
black by black technically black mantanblack winter
black coolblack 360degreesblack coalblack midnight
black black when it's convenient rustyblack moonblack
black starblack summerblack electronblack spaceman
black shoeshineblack jimshoeblack underwearblack ugly
black auntjimammablack, uncleben'srice black williebest
black blackisbeautifulblack i justdiscoveredblack negro
black unsubstanceblack.

and everywhere the
lady "negro poet"
appeared the poets were there.
they listened and questioned
& went home feeling uncomfortable/unsound & sountogether
they read/re-read/wrote & re-wrote
& came back the next time to tell the
lady "negro poet"

how beautiful she was/is & how she had helped them
& she came back with:
>how necessary they were and how they've helped her.
the poets walked & as space filled the vacuum between them & the
lady "negro poet"
u could hear one of the blackpoets say:
>"bro, they been calling that sister by the wrong name."


## MALCOLM SPOKE / who listened?

(this poem is for my consciousness too)

he didn't say
wear yr/blackness in
outer garments
& blk/slogans fr/the top 10.

he was fr a long
line of super-cools,
>doo-rag lovers &
>revolutionary pimps.
u are playing that
high-yellow game in blackface
minus the straighthair.
now
it's nappy-black
& air conditioned volkswagens
with undercover whi
te girls who studied faulkner at
smith
& are authorities on "militant"
knee/grows
selling u at jew town rates:
>niggers with wornout tongues
>three for a quarter/or will consider a trade
the double-breasted hipster
has been replaced with a
dashiki wearing rip-off
who went to city college
majoring in physical education.

animals come in all colors.
dark meat will roast as fast as whi-te meat
especially in
the unitedstatesofamerica's
new
self-cleaning ovens.

if we don't listen.


## SUN HOUSE

(a living legend)

his fingers leaned
forcefully against the neck
of a broken gin bottle
that
rubbed gently on
the steel strings of a borrowed guitar.

the roughness of his voice
is only matched by his immediate
presence that is lifted into
life with lonely words: "is u is or is u ain't
                    my baby, i say,
                    is u is or is u ain't
                    my baby, if u ain't
                    don't confess it now."

to himself he knew the answers
& the answers were amplified
by the sharpness of the broken bottle
that gave accent
to the muddy music as it screamed
& scratched the unpure lines
of our many faces,
while our bodies jumped to the sounds of

mississippi.

# WE WALK THE WAY OF THE NEW WORLD

1.

we run the dangercourse.
the way of the stocking caps & murray's grease.
(if u is modern u used duke greaseless hair pomade)
jo jo was modern/ an international nigger
                    born: jan. 1, 1863 in new york, mississippi.
his momma was mo militant than he was/is
jo jo bes no instant negro
his development took all of 106 years
& he was the first to be stamped "made in USA"
where he arrived bow-legged a curve ahead of the 20th
        century's new weapon: television.
which invented, "how to win and influence people"
& gave jo jo his how/ever look: however u want me.

we discovered that with the right brand of cigarettes
that one, with his best girl,
cd skip thru grassy fields in living color
& in slow-motion: Caution: niggers, cigarette smoking
                    will kill u & yr/health.
& that the breakfast of champions is: blackeyed peas & rice.
& that God is dead & Jesus is black and last seen on 63rd
            street in a gold & black dashiki, sitting in a pink
            hog speaking swahili with a pig-latin accent.
& that integration and coalition are synonymous,
& that the only thing that really mattered was:
        who could get the highest on the least or how to expand
        & break one's mind.

in the coming world
new prizes are
to be given
we *ran* the dangercourse.
now, it's a silent walk/ a careful eye
jo jo is there
to his mother he is unknown
(she accepted with a newlook: what wd u do if someone
        loved u?)

jo jo is back
& he will catch all the new jo jo's as they wander in & out
and with a fan-like whisper say: you ain't no
                              tourist
                              and Harlem ain't for
                              sight-seeing, brother.

        2.

Start with the itch and there will be no scratch. Study
        yourself.
Watch yr/every movement as u skip thru-out the southside of
        chicago.
be hip to yr/actions.


our dreams are realities
traveling the nature-way.
we meet them
at the apex of their utmost
meanings/means;
we walk in cleanliness
down state st/or Fifth Ave.
& wicked apartment buildings shake
as their windows announce our presence
as we jump into the interior
& cut the day's evil away.

We walk in cleanliness
the newness of it all
becomes us
our women listen to us
and learn.
We teach our children thru
our actions.

We'll become owners of the        New World
the New World.
will run it as unowners
for
we will live in it too
& will want to be remembered
as       realpeople.

# SHERLEY ANNE WILLIAMS

## (B. 1944)

*The poems of Sherley Anne Williams are often based in or derived from, existentially speaking, the blues, which is to say that they go beyond the structure and content rules of that form into a sense of the blues as a way of seeing the world, as a way of life. Comments that Williams has made about her second book,* Some One Sweet Angel Chile, *could apply to all of her work, a "series of self-affirmations, each rooted in a sense of the sisterhood of black women and dealing with some aspect of self-image. Each arises out of a deeper and wider sense of the group experience." She has also stated that her poems have dealt in "a kind of contrary innocence because it is maintained in the face of what [a poetic persona] knows the world thinks is her place." Ms. Williams's poems are technically exquisite, fully controlled, and thoroughly imagined, dealing with subject matter that could be trite or maudlin with truth, humor, and a lack of pathos. Sherley Anne Williams grew up in Fresno, California, graduating from California State University at Fresno. She then studied at Fisk and Howard universities before earning a master's degree at Brown. She has published several books, as well as stories, criticism, and a play. She lives in California and teaches at the University of California at San Diego.*

## LETTERS FROM
## A NEW ENGLAND NEGRO

> . . . and every member rejoiced
>    in a single segment made whole
>       with the circle
>          in the recognition
>             of a single voice . . .

Mrs. Josiah Harris
No. 5 The Grange Street
Newport, Rhode Island

August 25, 1867

Dear Miss Nettie,

The School is in a spinney
down behind the old Quarters
where many of the freedmen
live. The teachers, myself
included, live in the Big
House, which—thus far!—has stirred
little comment among the
local whites.

The School is the largest
public building in which blacks
and whites can safely congregate.
Sunday services are held there
and many of the freedmen
attend. Miss Esther introduced
me to several as "the
herald of Emancipation's
new day."

They murmured discreetly
among themselves, the women
smiling quickly, the men
nodding or cutting their
eyes toward me. Finally an
older man stepped forward, "I'm is
Peter, Miss Patient Herald,"
he said, pumping my hand. Then,
with great satisfaction,
"Lotsa room in the Big House.
                              Now."

Mr. Edward Harris
5 The Grange Street
Newport, Rhode Island

August 25, 1867

Edward, I do know <u>some</u> of
whom they speak, especially
the ones now dead, Pope and Homer,
though I cannot read the Greek;
such discussions are the dreams
I dreamed myself in that one
short year at school. But Homer,
as you warned, does not so often
figure in conversation
as I had supposed.

I nod
and smile as Miss Nettie bade
me, but my silence is more
noticeable here than at
her table. I have told my
tale of meeting Emerson
while a servant for the Straights;
they have marveled at that lucky
fate. And only after the
moment passes do I
remember the humorous
exchange between some children
or my comical fright at
walking through the spinney.

We sit on the veranda
most evenings and sometimes Beryl
consents to play for us. The
Old Nights gather then in this
southern dusk: Mistress at the
piano, light from twin
candelabra bringing
color to her cheeks, French doors
open to the darkness;
listeners sitting quietly
in the heat.

Now and then
beneath the country airs that
are Beryl's specialty comes a
snatch of melody such as
no mistress ever played and
I am recalled to the present
place. Freedmen sing here now. It
is Cassie or Miss Esther who
turns the music's page. Or myself.


Miss Ann Spencer
Lyme on Eaton
New Strowbridge, Connecticut

August 30, 1867

Dear Ann,

Caution is not so necessary
here as in some other parts
of the state, but we hear of
the "night-riding" and terror
and so are careful. Yet, Miss
Esther's bearing is such that
she is accorded grudging
civility by even
rabid Rebels and though there
was at first some muttering
at young white women teaching

"nigras," Cassie and Beryl are
likewise accepted; thus the
School escapes reprisals.

And,
if the local ladies lift
their skirts aside as I pass—
Well, perhaps I <u>should</u> smirch them.
If my cast-off clothes are
thought unsuited to my station,
my head held too high as I
step back to let the meanest white
go before me, why—What then
is a concert in Newport
or a day in Boston compared
to the chance to be arrogant
amongst so many southerners!

September 9, 1867

Dear Edward,

The children, I am told, had
little notion of order
and none of <u>school</u>. The first months
here, by all accounts, were
hectic. New students came daily
and changed their names almost
as often, or came and went
at will and those that stayed, talked
throughout the lesson.

They sit
now as prim as Topsy must
have done when first confronted
with Miss Ophelia, hands
folded neatly, faces lit
with pious expectancy.
We teach them to read and write
their names, some basic sums and
talk to them of Douglass and
Tubman and other heroes
of the race.

They are bright
enough—as quick as any
I taught in Newport. Yet behind
their solemn stares, I sense a
game such as I played with those
mistresses who tried to teach
me how best to do the very
task for which I had been
especially recommended,
and so suspect that what we
call learning is in them mere
obedience to some rules.


*October 22, 1867*

The girls are bold, fingering
our dresses, marveling at
our speech. They cluster around
us at recess, peppering
us with questions about the
North and ourselves. Today, one
asked why I did not cover
my head or at least braid my
hair as is decent around
white folk. We do not speak of
hair in the north, at least in
public, and I answered sharply,
It is not the custom in
the North and I am from the
North—meaning, of course, that I
am freeborn.

I know how
chancy freedom is among
us and so have never
boasted of my birth. And
they were as much stung by my

retort as I by their question.
But in the moment of my
answer the scarves worn by the
women seemed so much a symbol
of our slavery that I would
have died before admitting
my childhood's longing for just
such patient plaiting of my
tangled hair or cover now
my wild and sullen head.


November 10, 1867

Dear Miss Nettie,

My group numbers twenty, aged
four through sixteen, now that
harvest is done. There are no
grades, of course, and Tuesday
nights I take a group of grown-ups
over the lessons I give the
youngsters the following week.

The
grown-ups are more shy with me
than with Miss Esther and the
others, seldom speaking unless
I have done so first and then
without elaboration.

I did not expect immediate
kinship as Beryl chides: I am
as stiff with them as they with
me; yet, in unguarded moments,
I speak as they do, softly
a little down in the throat
muting the harsh gutterals and
strident diphthongs on my tongue.

*November 24, 1867*

There was in Warwick Neck, at
the time we lived there, a black
woman named Miss Girt whose aunt
had bought her out of slavery
in the District some fifty
years before. She was a
familiar and striking figure
in that town where there were few
negroes; of that color we
called smoothblack—a dense and
even tone that seems to drink
the light. The strawberry pink
of her mouth spilled over onto
the darkness of her lips and
a sliver of it seemed to
cut the bottom one in two.

She kept a boarding house for
negroes, mostly men who worked
at odd jobs up and down the
Coast. The white children whispered
about it—though the house
differed only in being
set in a larger plot with
two or three vacant ones between
it and its nearest neighbors.
It was the closest thing to
a haunted house the town provided
and on idle afternoons
the white children "dared
the boogey man"—though they seldom
got close enough to disturb
Miss Girt or her boarders with
their rude calls and flourishes—
and withdrew giggling and
pushing at the slightest
movement or noise.

We went also,
on our infrequent trips
to town, to see the boogey
man and sometimes heard a strain
of music, a sudden snatch
of laughter. Or watched the white
children from a distance. Once
George Adam called out, "Here She
come," sending them into clumsy
flight and us into delighted
laughter. Once Miss Girt herself
came round the corner on the
heels of their cry, "Nigger!"

"And
a free one, too," she called and
laughed at their startled silence.
They fled in disorder,
routed, so George said, by the
boldness of this sally, and,
I thought, by the hot pink in
the laughing dark of Miss Girt's face.

December 15, 1867

Edward dearest,

They persist in calling me
Patient though I have tried to
make it clear that neither
Emancipation nor Patience
is part of my given name.
They understand the Herald
part and laugh at Peter who
says he could not then understand
that New England talk. The
following week, I am again
Miss Patient Hannah. I tell
myself, it is not so important
and truly have ceased to argue,
have come indeed to still any
impulse to retort almost
as it is born.

Tonight my
old devil tongue slipped from
me after weeks of careful
holding. I answered roughly
some harmless question, My name
is Hannah. Hannah. There is
no Patience to it.

"Hannah
our name for the sun," Stokes said
in the silence that followed
my remark. "You warm us like
she do, but you more patient
wid us when we come to learn."


*December 27, 1867*

The men play their bodies like
drums, their mouths and noses like
wind instruments, creating
syncopated rhythms, wild
melodies that move the people
to wordless cries as they dance.
There are true musicians—Givens
who plays the banjo, Lloyd the
fiddler, many singers. Even
the tamborinists and those
who shake the bones coax beauty
from nothingness and desire.
Yet it is the music of
those who play themselves, that tone
half voice, half instrument that
echoes in my head. Tonight at
Stokes' wedding I was moved by
this to moan and dance myself.

January 5, 1868

My dear,

Beryl sees the poverty of my
childhood as a dim reflection
of the slavery in which
Pansy lived, sees in her, as
indeed in all, some vestige
of my former self that teaching
frees me of.

I see in her,
too, some other Pansy, some
Other, not my self and not
so simple as we thought her.

We have come among Christians
for whom Dance is the crossing
of the feet; what they do not
know of the world is learnable.
It is this I have come to
teach. Beryl has no eye for such
distinctions, seeing only
frenzy where I have been taught
the speech of walk and shout.

January 12, 1868

Dear Miss Nettie,

The school stands now where the praise
grove was; the grass then was worn
away by bended knees, the
dirt packed hard by shouting feet.

"Go wid Massa, Lawd; go wid
Massa."

Pansy mimics the
old prayer, torso going
in one direction, limbs in
some other. There is laughter,
murmurs of "Do, Lawd" and "Amen."
But it is memory she
dances; the praise grove was gone
before the War, closed by the
Masters' fears.

"Dey ain trus mo'n
one darky alone wid Chris;
two darkies togetha need
a <u>live</u> white man near."

Pansy's
mother and many others
gathered then in twos and threes
in secret clearings in the
woods, quiet witness that
our Savior lives.

"Go wid
Massa, Jesus. Go <u>wid</u> dis
white man.

"And Mista Lincoln
                        did."

Their triumph is renewed
in our laughter, yet there are
some—Pansy I think is one—
who scoff at white men's ways and
gather now in the same hushed
harbors to worship and to
whisper of the new jesus
in the old praise grove's heart.

*January 21, 1868*

She comes grudgingly
to know the world
within the printed
page yet rejoices
in Stokes' progress

She trusts the power
of the word only
as speech and sets me
riddles whose answers
I cannot speak

How
do the white man school
you
*Give a nigga*
*a hoe*

How do he
control you
*Put a*
*mark on some paper*
*turn our chi'ren to*

*noughts*
How do master
tell darkies apart
*By looking at the*
*lines and dots*

I tell
myself it is the
catechism of
unlettered negroes
that one dance has made

me Darky; pagan
and half wild.
She is
as black and lovely
as her namesake's heart

and teases me about
my "learnin"
She would
row my head with seed
plaits And prays I have
not been ruined by

this white man's schooling.

February 7, 1868

Edward,

I may attend prayer meetings
in the Quarters, go now
and then to the services "Singing"
Johnson leads. If such as
Sister Jones or Mrs. Casper from
the town ask, I may go to
gatherings in their homes. And
I am free to go wherever
Cassie and Beryl are invited.
Thus my need for company
is understood and addressed;
so, I am not to go to
play parties in the Quarters
nor go there of an evening
to Stokes' and Pansy's to talk
and listen at the music and
the tales. Miss Esther is shocked
that I would even consider
such actions without seeking
advice from Beryl or Cassie
or go without asking leave
of herself. It is a stalemate:
she will not give her permission;
I go and ask no one's consent.

February 15, 1868

I know you are not wholly
knowledgeable of all I
write you, dearest Ann, yet your
own eccentricity at
times allows you to apprehend
what most would miss. And I do
not expect answers or advice.
We stand outside each other's
lives and are enchanted with this
unlikely meeting: the blue-
stockinged white lady, the smart
colored girl. I stand now
outside the life I know as
negro. Sometimes, as I try
to make sensible all that
I would tell you, I see my
self as no more than a
recorder and you a listening
ear in some future house.


March 3, 1868

Dearest One,

I have no clear recall of
how I came to be at the
door of my first mistress, kept
little of that beginning, save
that through bargaining I fixed
my wage and worked extra for
room and board. I cannot now
remember all the helping
hands I passed through before the
Harrises took me in. There are
things I tell no one and have
ceased to tell myself. I have
grown to womanhood with my past
almost a blank.

I do not
recall, yet the memory
colors all that I am. I
know only that I was a
servant; now my labor is
returned to me and all my
waiting is upon myself.

■

# RALPH DICKEY

(1945–1972)

*Michael S. Harper has described the late Ralph Dickey as a "crafts-
man of [a] deep image of the spirit," utilizing "an overall conception
of mystery, language, and the force-field of the word." Though his
enormous promise was cut tragically short, Mr. Dickey exhibited in
his brief career an acute ear for language and a gift for strange and
wonderful images that is equally indebted to the American Robert
Hayden and such German-language poets as Paul Celan and Georg
Trakl. Ralph Dickey was born in Detroit, Michigan, and was educated
at Montieth College of Wayne State University in Detroit and the
University of Iowa. An accomplished musician and composer, he died
in 1972, by his own hand.*

## FATHER

I sat on my stool
in the dark
a plane of light
from the cracked door
fell across my face
like a burn
in the next room
my father was beating

my mother to death
he kicked her until
she cried blood
and then he kicked her
until she came down
with a coma
and then he kicked her until
he just couldn't
kick her no more
he came in to see me
and put his hand on
my shoulder listen
I want you to kill
a man for me
I stood up he shoved me
back sit down I'll
give you a hundred
dollars what do you
say I said well
who is it
here's a piece of paper
with the man's name
kill him I'll give you
a hundred dollars
I opened the paper my name
was on it I turned
it over to see if
there was an alternate
what is this I said
some kind of goddam
joke I never joke
about money
he said


## MULATTO LULLABY

Be my stillborn son my son
so the doctors will haul you
out to the world
and whip your skin to suede

Be my stillborn son my son
so the flies will land
on your wet glass eyes
and wade like cranes

Be my stillborn son my son
so the flies will deposit
their pouches of maggots
mouthfuls of rice

Son born stillborn
float in the jar
like you soaked in my womb


## LEAVING EDEN

Named and unnamed and renamed
armed and unarmed and disarmed
I have my covenant outside the womb
in the solitary confinement of my cells

The cries of my bones
like the cries of animals
followed me out of my mother
into exile

# CALVIN FORBES

## (B. 1945)

*The quiet gentility—genteel as a compliment—of the poems of Cal-*
*vin Forbes masks many virtues—control, vocabulary, learning—*
*about which other poets and poems shout. This reticence, in his case,*
*only makes his work more appealing. Mr. Forbes writes about family,*
*history, and music in ways that illustrate a strong understanding of*
*and connection with both American and African-American tradition,*
*but not without making these often disparate influences his own.*

## MY FATHER'S HOUSE
1908–1970

I live quietly and go nowhere
And this house shakes like a tree.
Open the door, Jesus is the hinge
Squeaking from the rusty rain.

Deadheart, this house wasn't built
By human hands, and no bricks will
You find, wood or glass. This house
Stands like a skeleton inside the worst

Possible skin. Knock and enter afraid,
Your shadow rigid as the brass laid
Across your coffin. Come closer and see
Broken beams, a sacred slum, no mystery

Except memory. Rise and make ends meet
My tenant. Safe in its vastness, retreat
To a hidden corner; without mercy guard
Its secret life as if a fortune were yours.

## BLUE MONDAY

Cotton eyes soaking up blood

All alone in Eskimo city
Cold and unsure, the music man

No earth angel, no sissy, brings
The night to its knees. Some-
Times he feels he's been below deck

All his life chained to a stranger
Moaning blue monday where's a calendar

Without weekends. Blue monday he moans
Where's a place where the darkness
Is not a dungeon. Slipping sliding his way

To be alive, he mumbles to his boss.
His soul trails behind him like a sled.

Too weak to work he's tired of playing.

He's gonna rock on the river of time
And stare at God until he goes blind.


## READING WALT WHITMAN

I found his wool face, I went away
A crook; there were lines I followed
When his song like a whistle led me.

Daily my wooden words fell, a parade
Of sticks, a broom bent over a thief's
Head. But then along came Langston

The proper shepherd who sat on history
Missing our music, dividing me; after
His death I rewrote, I robbed, and hid

In a foxhole until my lines were wood
On top, and soft underneath the bark.
Good Langston sat too long to lift me.

■

# MARILYN NELSON WANIEK

## (B. 1946)

*Marilyn Nelson Waniek is capable of writing in different styles and voices about a wide range of subjects. Primarily a poet of the family and interested in probing its internal and external links, Ms. Waniek has written well about other things—penguins, Emily Dickinson, jazz—whatever seems to gain the attention of her curious intelligence. Her Tuskegee Airmen sequence is a special achievement, as she explores her father's life in the army and in so doing brings to light poetically a great moment in American history, when blacks were allowed to be military pilots. Marilyn Nelson Waniek was born in Cleveland and educated at the universities of California at Davis, Pennsylvania, and Minnesota. She is the author of three books of poems and the recipient of two NEA Fellowships. She lives in Connecticut, where she is a professor at the state university.*

## MY GRANDFATHER
## WALKS IN THE WOODS

Somewhere
in the light above the womb,
black trees
and white trees
populate a world.

It is a March landscape,
the only birds around are small
and black.
What do they eat,
sitting in the birches
like warnings?

The branches of the trees
are black and white.
Their race is winter.
They thrive in cold.

There is my grandfather
walking among the trees.
He does not notice
his fingers are cold.
His black felt hat
covers his eyes.

He is knocking on each tree,
listening to their voices
as they answer slowly
deep, deep from their roots.
I am John, he says,
are you my father?

They answer
with voices like wind
blowing away from him.


## EMILY DICKINSON'S DEFUNCT

She used to
pack poems
in her hip pocket.
Under all the
gray old lady
clothes she was
dressed for action.
She had hair,
imagine,
in certain places, and
believe me
she smelled human
on a hot summer day.
Stalking snakes
or counting
the thousand motes
in sunlight
she walked just
like an Indian.

She was New England's
favorite daughter,
she could pray
like the devil.
She was a
two-fisted woman,
this babe.
All the flies
just stood around
and buzzed
when she died.


## FREEMAN FIELD

*For Edward Wilson Woodward, Captain
USAF (ret.) and the 101 of the 477th*

It was a cool evening
in the middle of April.
The 477th, the only Negro
bombadier group in the Air Corps,
had just been transferred
to Freeman Field.

Some of the guys
said they were hungry
and left to find food.
The others went on
playing bridge,
mending socks,
writing letters home.

A few minutes later
the hungry guys came back,
still hungry.
*We're under arrest.*

The others thought they were kidding.

The next morning
the Base Commander
issued new regulations:
Negro officers were assigned
to the NCO Club;
white officers were assigned
to the Officers' Club.

The Base Commander,
who had deliberately busted
an entire Negro outfit
so he wouldn't have to be
their flight-leader in combat,
was a graduate of West Point.

He issued a statement:
*If we do not allow*
*Negro and white officers to mix,*
*the accident rate*
*will go down two*
*and two-tenths*
*percent.*

Sixty-one Negro officers
were ordered to report
one by one
to his office.
*Lieutenant, have you read the regulations?*
*Sign here if you have read and understood.*

Sixty-one Negro officers
refused to sign.
*A man of your intelligence*
*must be able to recognize*
*the dangers of fraternization.*

They refused to sign.
*This is an order:*
*Sign the document.*

They refused to sign.
*This is a direct order!*
*You will sign the document!*

Six cargo planes were called in;
pilots, navigators, and bombadiers
were shoved on board and flown
to Godman Field, Kentucky.

Across the river
was Fort Knox.
The sixty-one
had grown by now
to one hundred and one
American fliers trained
to fight Nazis.
They were confined
to the BOQ
under guard
of armed MP's.

By night, searchlights watched
every window. By daylight
the men leaned in the windows
to smoke, watching
the German POW's pump gas,
wash windshields
and laugh
at the motorpool
across the street.

## THREE MEN IN A TENT

*For Rufus C. Mitchell*

My one blood-uncle laughs
and shakes his handsome head.
*Yeah, that was Ol' Corbon.*
*He was your daddy's classmate,*
*you know: They went to school together*
*at Wilberforce.*

Seemed like Ol' Corbon
was in trouble all the time.
We slept two guys to a tent,
you know, and seemed like nobody
wanted to bunk with Ol' Corbon.
He was such a hard-luck case;
the guys thought he was jinxed.

Finally, he came to me and Dillard
—Dillard was my tent-mate—
and asked if he could bunk with us,
because he knew your dad.
He said he'd sleep
at the foot of our tent.
Dillard said, *Shit, man,*
but I talked him over.

We were on Cape Bon, Tunisia,
you know, and we had to take turns
doing guard-duty.
The Germans parachuted soldiers in
almost every night,
and they knifed men
sleeping in their tents.

One night it was Ol' Corbon's turn,
and he fell asleep on duty.
You know,
you can be shot
for that during combat.
But Ol' Corbon bailed himself out;
he bought life
with his black mother-wit.

The water there
was corroding the cooling systems.
If they rusted too much,
the planes couldn't fly.
Most of the pilots
—Negro and white—
were just sitting around.
The ground-crews were going crazy,
but what could we do?

You had to use water,
and the corrosive water
was the only water we had.

Then Ol' Corbon remembered
that they'd had to build a distillery
to make distilled water
for the chemistry lab at Wilberforce.
*Hey, man,* he told me,
*I think we can do that.*
So we rag-patched one together
and got our boys
back in the air.

The Commanding Officer came over
to find out why the colored boys could fly,
and Ol' Corbon explained our distillery.

Then there were the spark-plug cleaners.
You know, it's easy in the States
to clean spark plugs:
you just use a spark-plug cleaner.
But we didn't have spark-plug cleaners;
they were back in the States.
The planes were grounded again
while we waited.
Thirty to sixty days,
they said it would take.

But Ol' Corbon said
*Hey, man,*
*I bet we can make one.*
*You want to try?*

Well, it turns out
to be pretty simple
to make a spark-plug cleaner.
You just take a big can,
fill it with desert sand,
make a space at the top
for a spark plug,
and blast high-pressure air
through a hole in the side.

You know, the first time
I saw General Eisenhower
was when he flew in
to find out why
the 99th was flying.

The CO introduced Staff Sergeant Corbon.

A little while later
Cape Bon Airfield
was integrated.
We were five men to a tent:
one of us
to four
of them.

I sure missed
my old buddies.
I even missed
Ol' Corbon.


## LONELY EAGLES

> For Daniel "Chappie" James, General USAF
> and for the 332nd Fighter Group

Being black in America
was the Original Catch,
so no one was surprised
by 22:
The segregated airstrips,
separate camps.
They did the jobs
they'd been trained to do.

Black ground-crews kept them in the air;
black flight-surgeons kept them alive;
the whole Group removed their headgear
when another pilot died.

They were known by their names:
"Ace" and "Lucky,"
"Sky-hawk Johnny," "Mr. Death."
And by their positions and planes.
*Red Leader to Yellow Wing-man,*
*do you copy?*

If you could find a fresh egg
you bought it and hid it
in your dopp-kit or your boot
until you could eat it alone.
On the night before a mission
you gave a buddy
your hiding-places
as solemnly
as a man dictating
his will.
*There's a chocolate bar*
*in my Bible;*
*my whiskey bottle*
*is inside my bed-roll.*

In beat-up Flying Tigers
that had seen action in Burma,
they shot down three German jets.
They were the only outfit
in the American Air Corps
to sink a destroyer
with fighter planes.
Fighter planes with names
like "By Request."
Sometimes the radios
didn't even work.

They called themselves
"Hell from Heaven."
This Spookwaffe.
My father's old friends.

It was always
maximum effort:
A whole squadron
of brother-men
raced across the tarmac
and mounted their planes.

My tent-mate was a guy named Starks.
The funny thing about me and Starks
was that my air mattress leaked,
and Starks' didn't.
Every time we went up,
I gave my mattress to Starks
and put his on my cot.

One day we were strafing a train.
Strafing's bad news:
you have to fly so low and slow
you're a pretty clear target.
My other wing-man and I
exhausted our ammunition and got out.
I recognized Starks
by his red tail
and his rudder's trim-tabs.
He couldn't pull up his nose.
He dived into the train
and bought the farm.

I found his chocolate,
three eggs, and a full fifth
of his hoarded-up whiskey.
I used his mattress
for the rest of my tour.

It still bothers me, sometimes:
I was sleeping
on his breath.

# STAR-FIX

*For Melvin M. Nelson, Captain USAF (ret.)*
*(1917–1966)*

At his cramped desk
under the astrodome,
the navigator looks
thousands of light-years
everywhere but down.
He gets a celestial fix,
measuring head-winds;
checking the log;
plotting wind-speed,
altitude, drift
in a circle of protractors,
slide-rules, and pencils.

He charts in his Howgozit
the points of no alternate
and of no return.
He keeps his eyes on the compass,
the two altimeters, the map.
He thinks, *Do we have enough fuel?*
*What if my radio fails?*

He's the only Negro in the crew.
The only black flyer on the whole base,
for that matter. Not that it does:
this crew is a team.
Bob and Al, Les, Smitty, Nelson.

Smitty, who said once
after a poker game,
*I love you, Nelson.*
*I never thought I could love*
*a colored man.*
*When we get out of this man's Air Force,*
*if you ever come down to Tuscaloosa,*
*look me up and come to dinner.*

*You can come in the front door, too;*
*hell, you can stay overnight!*
*Of course, as soon as you leave,*
*I'll have to burn down my house.*
*Because if I don't*
*my neighbors will.*

The navigator knows where he is
because he knows where he's been
and where he's going.
At night, since he can't fly
by dead-reckoning,
he calculates his position
by shooting a star.

The octant tells him
the angle of a fixed star
over the artificial horizon.
His position in that angle
is absolute and true:
*Where the hell are we, Nelson?*
Alioth, in the Big Dipper,
Regulus. Antares, in Scorpio.

He plots their lines
of position on the chart,
gets his radio bearing,
corrects for lost time.

Bob, Al, Les, and Smitty
are counting on their navigator.
If he sleeps,
they all sleep.
If he fails
they fall.

The navigator keeps watch
over the night and the instruments,
going hungry for five or six hours
to give his flight-lunch
to his two little girls.

# PORTER

*For Bertram Wilson, Lieutenant Colonel
USAF (ret.) and for all of my "uncles"*

Suddenly
when I hear airplanes overhead—
big, silver ones
whose muscles fill the sky—
I listen: That sounds like
someone I know.
And the sky
looks much closer.

I know my intimacy, now,
with the wheel and roar
of wind around wings.
*Hello, wind.*
*Take care of my people.*
The moon and stars
aren't so white now;
some of my people
know their first names.
*Hey, Arcturus.*
*What's happening, Polaris?*
*Daddy said I should look you up.*

*You're even*
*more*
*dumb-founding*
*than he told me you were.*

This is my other heritage:
I have roots in the sky.
The Tuskegee Airmen
are my second family.
This new, brave,
decorated tribe.

My family.
My homeplace, at last.
It was there
all through time.
I only had
to raise my eyes.

Tuskegee Airmen,
uncles of my childhood,
how shall I live and work
to match your goodness?
Can I do more
than murmur name upon name,
as the daughter
of a thousand proud fathers?

Jefferson.
Wilson.
Sparks.
Toliver.
Woodward.
Mitchell.
Price.
Lacy.
Straker.
Smith.
Washington.
Meriweather.
White . . .

　　　One time, this was in the Sixties,
　　　and I was a full-bird Colonel,
　　　they called me in Kentucky
　　　and asked me to pick up
　　　an aircraft somebody had crashed
　　　down in Louisiana.
　　　I was supposed to fly it
　　　to a base in New Mexico
　　　and go back to Kentucky
　　　on a commercial flight.

It's tricky business,
flying a plane that's been crashed.
You can never tell
what might still be wrong with it.

Okay, I flew the plane to New Mexico
and got on a flight back home.
I was in full dress-uniform,
decorations and medals
and shit
all over my chest.
The Distinguished Flying Cross
with two Bronze Oak Leaf Clusters,
The Bronze Star,
a couple of commendation medals,
a European-African-Middle East Campaign Medal
with four Bronze Service Stars . . .

## TUSKEGEE AIRFIELD

*For the Tuskegee Airmen*

These men,
these proud black men:
our first to touch
their fingers to the sky.

The Germans learned to call them
*Die Schwarzen Vogelmenschen.*
They called themselves
*The Spookwaffe.*

Laughing.
And marching to class under officers
whose thin-lipped ambition
was to *wash the niggers out.*

Sitting at attention
for lectures about ailerons, airspeed, altimeters
from boring lieutenants who believed
*you monkeys ain't meant to fly.*

Oh, there were parties,
cadet-dances, guest appearances
by the Count
and the lovely Lena.

There was the embarrassing
adulation of Negro civilians.
A woman approached my father in a bar
where he was drinking with his buddies.
*Hello, Airman.* She held out her palm.
*Will you tell me my future?*

There was that,
like a breath of pure oxygen.
But first
they had to earn wings.

 There was this one instructor
 who was pretty nice.
 I mean, we just sat around
 and *talked* when a flight had gone well.

 But he was from Minnesota,
 and he made us sing
 the Minnesota Fight Song
 before we took off.

 If you didn't sing it,
 your days were numbered.
 "Minnesota, hats off to thee . . ."
 That bastard!

 One time I had a check-flight
 with an instructor from Louisiana.
 As we were about to head for base,
 he chopped the power.

 *Force-landing, nigger.*
 There were trees everywhere I looked.
 Except on that little island . . .
 I began my approach.

The instructor said, *Pull Up.*
*That was an excellent approach.*
Real surprised.
*But where would you have taken off, wise guy?*

I said, *Sir,*
*I was ordered*
*to land the plane.*
*Not take off.*

The instructor grinned.
*Boy, if your ass*
*is as hard as your head,*
*you'll go far in this world.*

■

# AI

## (B. 1947)

*The poems of Ai are almost always dramatic monologues, with the
poet assuming the voice of an estranged or dispossessed outsider,
equally likely to be a world personage like Leon Trotsky or an anony-
mous young black participant in the 1992 Los Angeles civil distur-
bance. With astonishing ventriloquism, Ai brings these voices to life,
providing brief moments of illumination to experiences that would
otherwise be ignored, overlooked, or forgotten. Her sympathies are
with those suffering in the world, and, as noted by Carolyn Forché,
she is skilled at "penetrating a social order which has become anes-
thetized to human agony." Ai was educated at the University of Ari-
zona and at the University of California at Irvine, and has taught at
several colleges. She is the author of five books of poetry; the second
of these,* Killing Floor, *received the 1979 Lamont Award.*

## CUBA, 1962

When the rooster jumps up on the windowsill
and spreads his red-gold wings,
I wake, thinking it is the sun
and call Juanita, hearing her answer,
but only in my mind.
I know she is already outside,
breaking the cane off at ground level,
using only her big hands.
I get the machete and walk among the cane,
until I see her, lying face-down in the dirt.

Juanita, dead in the morning like this.
I raise the machete—
what I take from the earth, I give back—
and cut off her feet.
I lift the body and carry it to the wagon,
where I load the cane to sell in the village.
Whoever tastes my woman in his candy, his cake,
tastes something sweeter than this sugar cane;
it is grief.
If you eat too much of it, you want more,
you can never get enough.


## RIOT ACT, APRIL 29, 1992

I'm going out and get something.
I don't know what.
I don't care.
Whatever's out there, I'm going to get it.
Look in those shop windows at boxes
and boxes of Reeboks and Nikes
to make me fly through the air
like Michael Jordan
like Magic.
While I'm up there, I see Spike Lee.
Looks like he's flying too
straight through the glass
that separates me
from the virtual reality
I watch every day on TV.

I know the difference between
what it is and what it isn't.
Just because I can't touch it
doesn't mean it isn't real.
All I have to do is smash the screen,
reach in and take what I want.
Break out of prison.
South Central homey's newly risen
from the night of living dead,
but this time he lives,
he gets to give the zombies
a taste of their own medicine.
Open wide and let me in,
or else I'll set your world on fire,
but you pretend that you don't hear.
You haven't heard the word is coming down
like the hammer of the gun
of this black son, locked out of the big house,
while massa looks out the window and sees only smoke.
Massa doesn't see anything else,
not because he can't,
but because he won't.
He'd rather hear me talking about mo' money,
mo' honeys and gold chains
and see me carrying my favorite things
from looted stores
than admit that underneath my Raider's cap,
the aftermath is staring back
unblinking through the camera's lens,
courtesy of CNN,
My arms loaded with boxes of shoes
that I will sell at the swap meet
to make a few cents on the declining dollar.
And if I destroy myself
and my neighborhood
"ain't nobody's business, if I do,"
but the police are knocking hard
at my door
and before I can open it,
they break it down
and drag me in the yard.

They take me in to be processed and charged,
to await trial,
while Americans forget
the day the wealth finally trickled down
to the rest of us.


## SELF DEFENSE

*For Marion Barry*

Y'all listen to me.
Why can't I get a witness?
Why can't I testify?
You heard the bitch. You heard her say
I can't even caress her breast.
Unless I smoke for sex,
I get next to nothing.
I get set up for spread thighs.
I am the mayor of Washington, D.C.
and I can be as nasty as I wanta.
You think you can chew me up
and spit me down in the gutter,
but I am there already.
I have no other choice.
I am a victim of the white press,
but I have the antidote for all your poison.
The rock of this age is crack
and like the primal urge to procreate,
desire for it surges through you,
until you praise its name
in the same breath as you do Jesus.
The need seizes addicts and lifts them to heaven
by the scruff of the neck,
then hurls them back,
drops in my lap a slut
who wouldn't even squeeze my nuts
for old times sake,
but made me puff that substitute,
until you FBI came bursting in.
Now I'm sure you think you should have shot me,

should have pretended I pulled a gun
and to defend yourselves, you had to do it.
You could have been through with it.
I could have been just another statistic.
I *am* realistic.
I am a man condemned for his weakness.
Had I been white,
I would have been the object of sympathy, not ridicule.
Trick me? Convict me?
Now, now you know
I'm not a man you can control.
The good ole days of slaves out pickin' cotton
ain't coming back no more. No,
with one drag, I took my stand against injustice.
Must a man give up his vices
because he is the mayor?
You made me a scapegoat,
one black man against the mistah massa race.
You thought I would cave in
and take my whuppin',
take my place
back of the endless soupline of the nineteen nineties,
as if it were still the fine and white fifties,
where y'all drink tea in the parlor
and the colored maids don't get no farther
than the next paycheck,
the next hand me downs from Mrs. so and so.
Po' ole mammies, po' ole black Joes,
working for low wages.
You don't need to quote my rights to me.
Don't they stick in your throat? Don't they?
All that marching and riding,
even torching Watts and Cleveland
gave us the right to vote,
but reading rights won't make a difference
if the verdict is already in.
You can't depend on nothing.
You got to toughen yourself.
I paid for my slice of American pie,
but you lie and say I stole it.
That is how you hold the nigger down
and beat him to death with his own freedom.

# ENDANGERED SPECIES

The color of violence is black.
Those are the facts, spreadeagled
against a white background,
where policemen have cornered the enemy,
where he shouldn't be, which is seen.
Of course, they can't always believe their eyes,
so they have to rely on instinct,
which tells them I am incapable
of civilized behavior,
therefore, I am guilty
of driving through my own neighborhood
and must take my punishment
must relax and enjoy
like a good boy.
If not, they are prepared to purge me
of my illusions of justice, of truth,
which is indeed elusive,
much like Sasquatch,
whose footprints and shit
are only the physical evidence
of what cannot be proved to exist,
much like me,
the "distinguished" professor of lit,
pulled from my car,
because I look suspicious.
My briefcase, filled with today's assignment
could contain drugs,
instead of essays arranged
according to quality of content,
not my students' color of skin,
but then who am I to say
that doesn't require a beating too?—
a solution that leaves no confusion
as to who can do whatever he wants to whom,
because there is a line directly
from slave to perpetrator,
to my face staring out of newspapers and TV,
or described over and over as a black male.
I am deprived of my separate identity
and must always be a race instead of a man

going to work in the land of opportunity,
because slavery didn't really disappear.
It simply put on a new mask
and now it feeds off fear
that is mostly justified,
because the suicides of the ghetto
have chosen to take somebody with them
and it may as well be you
passing through fire,
as I'm being taught
that injustice is merely another way
of looking at the truth.
At some point, we will meet
at the tip of the bullet,
the blade, or the whip
as it draws blood,
but only one of us will change,
only one of us will slip
past the captain and crew of this ship
and the other submit to the chains
of a nation
that delivered rhetoric
in exchange for its promises.

# YUSEF KOMUNYAKAA

## (B. 1947)

*The poems of Yusef Komunyakaa are deeply felt and experienced, often narrating the author's memory of childhood, his time in Vietnam, or an emotion—often melancholy—that is salved by music and/or love. Gifted with a strong vocabulary and a musical sense of language, Mr. Komunyakaa can navigate the most gentle moments, and his poems are, at their best, both moving and truth-telling. Yusef Komunyakaa was born in Louisiana, and served in Vietnam as a war correspondent. He has taught at Indiana University, and currently lives in Berkeley, California.*

# UNTITLED BLUES

after a photograph by Yevgeni Yevtushenko

I catch myself trying
to look into the eyes
of the photo, at a black boy
behind a laughing white mask
he's painted on. I
could've been that boy
years ago.
Sure, I could say
everything's copacetic,
listen to a Buddy Bolden cornet
cry from one of those coffin-
shaped houses called
shotgun. We could
meet in Storyville,
famous for quadroons,
with drunks discussing God
around a honky-tonk piano.
We could pretend we can't
see the kitchen help
under a cloud of steam.
Other lurid snow jobs:
night & day, the city
clothed in her see-through
French lace, as pigeons
coo like a beggar chorus
among makeshift studios
on wheels—Vieux Carré
belles having portraits painted
twenty years younger.
We could hand jive
down on Bourbon & Conti
where tap dancers hold
to their last steps,
mammy dolls frozen
in glass cages. The boy
locked inside your camera,
perhaps he's lucky—
he knows how to steal

laughs in a place
where your skin
is your passport.

## ELEGY FOR THELONIOUS

Damn the snow.
Its senseless beauty
pours a hard light
through the hemlock.
Thelonious is dead. Winter
drifts in the hourglass;
notes pour from the brain cup.
Damn the alley cat
wailing a muted dirge
off Lenox Ave.
Thelonious is dead.
Tonight's a lazy rhapsody of shadows
swaying to blue vertigo
& metaphysical funk.
Black trees in the wind.
*Crepuscule with Nellie*
plays inside the bowed head.
"Dig the Man Ray of piano!"
O Satisfaction,
hot fingers blur
on those white rib keys.
*Coming on the Hudson.*
*Monk's Dream.*
The ghost of bebop
from 52nd Street,
footprints in the snow.
Damn February.
Let's go to Minton's
& play "modern malice"
till daybreak. Lord,
there's Thelonious
wearing that old funky hat
pulled down over his eyes.

# HOW I SEE THINGS

I hear you were
sprawled on the cover of *Newsweek*
with freedom marchers, those years
when blood tinted the photographs,
when fire leaped into the trees.

Negatives of nightriders
develop in the brain.
The Strawberry Festival Queen
waves her silk handkerchief,
executing a fancy high kick

flashback through the heart.
Pickups with plastic Jesuses
on dashboards head for hoedowns.
Men run twelve miles into wet cypress
swinging bellropes. Ignis fatuus can't be blamed

for the charred Johnson grass.
Have we earned the right
to forget, forgive
ropes for holding
to moonstruck branches?

Every last stolen whisper
the hoot owl echoes
turns leaves scarlet.
Hush shakes the monkeypod
till pink petal-tongues fall.

You're home in New York.
I'm back here in Bogalusa
with one foot in pinewoods.
The mockingbird's blue note
sounds to me like *please,*

*please.* A beaten song
threaded through the skull
by cross hairs.
Black hands still turn blood red
working the strawberry fields.

# FRAGGING

Five men pull straws
under a tree on a hillside.
Damp smoke & mist halo them
as they single out each other,
pretending they're not there.
"We won't be wasting a real man.
That lieutenant's too gung ho.
Think, man, 'bout how Turk
got blown away; next time
it's you or me. Hell,
the truth is the truth."
Something small as a clinch pin
can hold men together,
humming their one-word
song. Yes, just a flick
of a wrist & the whole night
comes apart. "Didn't we warn him?
That bastard." "Remember, Joe,
remember how he pushed Perez?"
The five men breathe like a wave
of cicadas, their bowed heads
filled with splintered starlight.
They uncoil fast as a fist.
Looking at the ground, four
walk north, then disappear. One
comes this way, moving through
a bad dream. Slipping a finger
into the metal ring, he's married
to his devil—the spoon-shaped
handle flies off. Everything
breaks for green cover,
like a hundred red birds
released from a wooden box.

# BETWEEN DAYS

Expecting to see him anytime
coming up the walkway
through blueweed & bloodwort,
she says, "That closed casket
was weighed down with stones."
The room is as he left it
fourteen years ago, everything
freshly dusted & polished
with lemon oil. The uncashed
death check from Uncle Sam
marks a passage in the Bible
on the dresser, next to the photo
staring out through the window.
"Mistakes. Mistakes. Now,
he's gonna have to give them this
money back when he gets home.
But I wouldn't. I would
let them pay for their mistakes.
They killed his daddy. & Janet,
she & her three children
by three different men, I hope
he's strong enough to tell her
to get lost. Lord, mistakes."
His row of tin soldiers
lines the window sill. The sunset
flashes across them like a blast.
She's buried the Silver Star
& flag under his winter clothes.
The evening's first fireflies
dance in the air like distant tracers.
Her chair faces the walkway
where she sits before the TV
asleep, as the screen dissolves
into days between snow.

# FACING IT

My black face fades,
hiding inside the black granite.
I said I wouldn't,
dammit: No tears.
I'm stone. I'm flesh.
My clouded reflection eyes me
like a bird of prey, the profile of night
slanted against morning. I turn
this way—the stone lets me go.
I turn that way—I'm inside
the Vietnam Veterans Memorial
again, depending on the light
to make a difference.
I go down the 58,022 names,
half-expecting to find
my own in letters like smoke.
I touch the name Andrew Johnson;
I see the booby trap's white flash.
Names shimmer on a woman's blouse
but when she walks away
the names stay on the wall.
Brushstrokes flash, a red bird's
wings cutting across my stare.
The sky. A plane in the sky.
A white vet's image floats
closer to me, then his pale eyes
look through mine. I'm a window.
He's lost his right arm
inside the stone. In the black mirror
a woman's trying to erase names:
No, she's brushing a boy's hair.

# FEBRUARY IN SYDNEY

Dexter Gordon's tenor sax
plays "April in Paris"
inside my head all the way back
on the bus from Double Bay.
*Round Midnight*, the '50s,
cool cobblestone streets
resound footsteps of Bebop
musicians with whiskey-laced voices
from a boundless dream in French.
Bud, Prez, Webster, & The Hawk,
their names run together riffs.
Painful gods jive talk through
bloodstained reeds & shiny brass
where music is an anesthetic.
Unreadable faces from the human void
float like torn pages across the bus
windows. An old anger drips into my throat,
& I try thinking something good,
letting the precious bad
settle to the salty bottom.
Another scene keeps repeating itself:
I emerge from the dark theatre,
passing a woman who grabs her red purse
& hugs it to her like a heart attack.
Tremolo. Dexter comes back to rest
behind my eyelids. A loneliness
lingers like a silver needle
under my black skin,
as I try to feel how it is
to scream for help through a horn.


# EUPHONY

Hands make love to thigh, breast, clavicle,
Willed to each other, to the keyboard—
Searching the whole forest of compromises
Till the soft engine kicks in, running

On honey. Dissonance worked
Into harmony, even-handed
As Art Tatum's plea to the keys.
Like a woman & man who have lived

A long time together, they know how
To keep the song alive. Wordless
Epics into the cold night, keepers
Of the fire—the right hand lifts

Like the ghost of a sparrow
& the left uses every motionless muscle.
Notes divide, balancing each other,
Love & hate tattooed on the fingers.

■

# GEORGE BARLOW

## (B. 1948)

*The best poems of George Barlow are concerned with family and his-
tory, and are written in lush and clear language that carries both emo-
tion and insight. Mr. Barlow was born and raised in northern
California, educated at Contra Costa College and California State
University at Hayward. He currently teaches at Grinnell College in
Iowa. His 1981 book,* Gumbo, *was selected by Ishmael Reed for the
National Poetry Series. He lives in Iowa City.*

## IN MY FATHER'S HOUSE

Always first to rise
he usually slipped into daybreak
like a phantom—heading
(in jacket jeans white socks & loafers)
for Alameda
the drowsy traffic
& buzzing electronics of Naval Air

But he plays a horn
& some mornings caught him
aching with jazz—reeling
in its chemistry & might:
Duke Bird Basie
riffs chords changes
softly grunted & mouthed
in his closet
in the hallway in
all the glory of the sunrise

Who knows what spirits
shimmer through the neurons
& acoustics of his sleep
before these mornings:
black Beethoven
shunning his own deafness
for the sake of symphony
a Haitian drummer—
eyes shut in the moonlight—
mounted by divine horsemen
who flash through his hands
pretty Billie
eating gardenias with a needle
singing the blues away

Maybe urges older than oceans
startle him in the shower
or in the livingroom
on his way out the door
compel him to swipe moments
from time he doesn't have
to inch notes across
pitiless lined sheets
that have waited on the piano all night
for beat & harmony to marry

On these mornings
he met the man with ease
didn't carry no heavy load
Car horns were trumpets
fog horns bassoons

train whistles blushing saxophones
On these mornings
he jammed with angels
popped his fingers
to music in his head
filled his great lungs
with cool air

## A DREAM OF THE RING:
## THE GREAT JACK JOHNSON

I'll be the first
to chase the white hope
from coast to coast
corner him at last
& buckle his knees
Rednecks in Reno
will check in their guns
& drop their ducats
to watch the sun gleam
from my teeth my dark muscles
my great bald head
Vamps & debs will blush & giggle
as they watch me train
will prance into paradise with me
carve their lives in my back
fan themselves
knead my heart like dough
Hate will snag me
jail me for crossing state lines
& being a man
I'll fight bulls in Madrid
Griots will feed me to their children
to make them strong
My jabs & hooks
sweat & knockouts
my derbies long cars & gall
will live forever
I'll have one rag of a time
when I become Jack Johnson

# CHRISTOPHER GILBERT

(B. 1948)

*The poems of Christopher Gilbert are unabashedly romantic, often exploring the polarities of joy and despair, but always with exuberant and sincere emotion. Mr. Gilbert is interested in many things, love, metaphysics, jazz, neighborhoods cosmic and local, and he embraces these interests with a vision and curiosity that are unflinching. Christopher Gilbert was born in Birmingham, Alabama, grew up in Detroit, and was educated at the University of Michigan, where he studied with Robert Hayden. His 1984 book,* **Across the Mutual Landscape,** *won the 1984 Walt Whitman Prize. He lives in Providence, Rhode Island, where he is a practicing psychologist.*

## THIS BRIDGE ACROSS

A moment comes to me
and it's a lot like the dead
who get in the way sometimes
hanging around, with their ranks
growing bigger by the second
and the game of tag they play
claiming whoever happens by.
I try to put them off
but the space between us
is like a country growing closer
which has a language I know
more and more of me is
growing up inside of, and
the clincher is the nothing
for me to do inside here
except to face my dead
as the spirits they are,
find the parts of me in them—
call them back with my words.
Ancestor worship or prayer?

It's a kind of getting by—
an extension of living
beyond my self my people taught me,
and each moment is a boundary
I will throw this bridge across.


## RESONANCE

In a back room
upstairs crouched over crystal
set, the dark headphones a cap
worn to finish the circuit.

Touching the quartz, a wave
would roll its clear tongue
against the windows, the dark
midwest faces came looking into—
spaces struck deep in the bone.

And I pulled the cat's whisker,
rolled the coil in hope,
from my hands a phoenix fluttered—
the lid of teenage body
a throbbing shell at sea.

Listening, I could hear
the whole Black house was music;
my brother playing Wes Montgomery downstairs
on the turntable, a lost double
octave rolling round through the air.


## AND, YES, THOSE SPIRITUAL
## MATTERS

*Elegy for Robert Hayden*

Whisper it,
"Oh Hayden,
he can do energy."

The words breaking in flower,
the breath on things
wearing bright new clothes.

The drums, bells, gods
in poemstate, speaking—
or hushin' each other.

The goofy dust
he threw in our tea materialized into
a story the class choked on.

Whisper it as he saw it—
intensely, the material part of being
is style.

Summons the Gabriel
half of him, the silent
leftover talk in your head.


## AFRICAN SCULPTURE

> After looking at figures from the Baluba tribe at the
> DeCordova Museum, June 1979, in Lincoln, Mass.
> The sculptures were on loan from Harvard's Fogg
> Museum where they were rarely available to the
> public.

I am staring out the window
'bout to think something; a nameless
spirit comes through the glass inevitable
as nightfall. This house against the breeze
angles dark as African sculpture
pouting in a museum exhibit.
In the distance silhouetted the ash tree
waves its hand of intricate fingers;
as I trace their bending routes I sense
the flutter of a black-winged bird
flush against my mind's back wall, flying
forward the way that time becomes distinct.

I wonder if it will land out there.
It waves its wing and my blood slowly
ripples. Suddenly, I am negative and it is
scene. I wonder what the pattern is of—
looking out the window at the stars,
my arms reach out to touch their darkest names.
I seem to be remembering something.
I'm about to speak. It might be
a bird's speech where the air is visible
as an old language rising up the throat of
wings, my arms mellow leaves leaning earthward—
but now the traffic outside gears up
and the tree no longer believes in me
and the bird flies off; a strange cold light
shoots its shiny axe thru the sky.

## A SORROW SINCE SITTING BULL

You sit in the back
of the pick-up, facing back,
with your reservation a skin
surrounding you, with a warm Bud
in your hand, with the where
the dirt road leads beneath you
spun up as the wheels spin around
till the present narrows to nothing
at the horizon.

For this sorrow all your relations
are ghosts in the truck with you,
and you ride on into the future,
facing back, facing back.

# NATHANIEL MACKEY

## (B. 1948)

*The poems of Nathaniel Mackey are startlingly original and complex. Marked by his unique sense of the line, they achieve their effects through dense layering and echo, and are capable of conveying intricate mixes of emotion and information. Nathaniel Mackey was born in Miami and moved, at a young age, to California, where he was raised and educated. His book of poems,* Eroding Witness, *was selected by Michael S. Harper for the National Poetry Series in 1985, and he is also the author of a book of fiction,* Bedouin Hornbook, *which is scheduled to be part of a larger work. He is a professor at the University of California, Santa Cruz, and is the editor of a magazine,* Hambone.

## WINGED ABYSS

*for Olivier Messiaen*

I wake up dreaming I'm forty years in
    back of the times,    hear talk of a
Bright Star converging on Egypt.
                        This on day
    two of this my thirty-fifth year,
forty years out in front that I
    even hear of it at all . . .


                  Such abrupt
fallings away of the ground, such obstructions
    like a cello with one string gone.
                    An avalanche of
    light. An old out-of-tune upright, some of
    whose keys keep getting stuck . . .
    A creaking door makes me dream of colors,
        caught up in whose warp a knotted
                      stick
    leaned on by the sun . . .

A war camp quartet for the end of time
        heard with ears whose time has yet to
                                begin . . .
    An unlikely music I hear makes a world
                                break
beyond its reach . . .


                So I wake up handed a book
        by an angel whose head has a rainbow
                                behind it.
        I wake up holding a book announcing the
                end of time.
                                A lullaby of wings, under-
            neath whose auspices, obedient, asleep
            with only one eye shut, not the
                                end of
the world but a bird at whose feet I hear
                                time
                                dissolve . . .


        A free-beating fist, each tip of wing turned
            inward. Battered gate of a City said to be
        of the Heart.
                            Held me up as if to cleanse me
            with fire, neither more nor less alive
                                than when
I wasn't there . . .


                I hear talk.
                            Out of touch
            with the times, I wake up asking what
                                bird
would make so awkward a
                sound

## DEGREE FOUR

—*"mu" seventh part*—


There though where they
were regardless,
elsewhere. Mat made of
  tossed-off straw.


 Tissuepaper
house worn atop the
head. Tissuepaper
    boat, lit up
                 inside . . .
  Vanishing thread,
bleached burlap
              sack . . .
  Took one step
forward, took
            two steps . . .


 Took to being taken
past the breaking
  point, muttered
                legless,
   "Hard light, be our
   witness," wondering why
     were they no match
                       for
drift.    Saw that this
was what history was, that
    thing they'd heard of.
  Ferried across Midnight
    Creek on a caiman's
                       back . . .
   Saw themselves made
     to eat uncooked rice . . .


 Kept in a room called
Búsinêngè Kámba, put
to work.    Saw this too
  was what history was.

                    Desolate
seedpod,      mother-in-law's
      tongue,      tongued rattle.
Footless romp, reflected
      light on flooded
ground . . .


                  Rolled a
joint with gunpowder
inside, struck a match,
whispered, "This is
    what history does."
Said, "Above sits
      atop its Below, each
    undoing the other
even though they
                        embrace."


  Went up in smoke, lit
by feathers of light,
    debris falling for
                        ages . . .
This as they thought,
    what was known as
history, this the
                        loaded
gun carried under their
                        coats . . .


  "Wooed by fish under
  shallow water . . ."
                        This
  too their sense of
    what history
                        was.
Fleeting glimpse of
    what, reached for,
                        faded,
  fickle sense of what,
  read with small sticks,
                        caved
in

# MELVIN DIXON

## (1950–1992)

*Melvin Dixon was a true man of letters, equally skilled at poetry, fiction, and criticism, and gifted with the energy to turn out copious amounts of work at a high level. As a poet, his preoccupations were with history, the African diaspora, family, and, as time went on, issues of homosexuality and the death specter of AIDS. Mr. Dixon was technically adept, influenced by Robert Hayden, Ralph Ellison, Jay Wright, and Michael S. Harper, and his early death was a significant blow to the promise of African-American literature. Melvin Dixon was born in Stamford, Connecticut, educated at Wesleyan and Brown universities, and taught at Fordham, Williams, Queens College, the City University of New York, and Columbia. He was the author of six books, numerous papers, articles, essays, and poems. He died of an AIDS-related illness in 1992.*

## TOUR GUIDE: *LA MAISON DES ESCLAVES*
Ile de Gorée, Senegal

He speaks of voyages:
men traveling spoon-fashion,
women dying in afterbirth,
babies clinging
to salt-dried nipples.
For what his old eyes still see
his lips have few words. Where
his flat thick feet still walk
his hands crack
into a hundred lifelines.

Here waves rush to shore
breaking news that we return
to empty rooms
where the sea is nothing calm.

And sun, tasting the skin
of black men,
leaves teeth marks.

The rooms are empty until he speaks.
His guttural French is a hawking trader.
His quick Wolof a restless warrior.
His slow, impeccable syllables
a gentleman trader. He tells
in their own language
what they have done.

Our touring maps and cameras ready
we stand in the weighing room
where chained men paraded firm backs,
their women open, full breasts,
and children,
rows of shiny teeth.

Others watched from the balcony,
set the price in guilders, francs,
pesetas and English pounds. Later
when he has finished we too
can leave our coins
where stiff legs dragged
in endless bargain.

He shows how some sat knee-bent
in the first room.
Young virgins waited in the second.
In the third, already red,
the sick and dying
gathered near the exit to the sea.

In the weighing room again
he takes a chain to show us
how it's done. We take
photographs to remember,
others leave coins to forget.
No one speaks
except iron on stone
and the sea
where nothing's safe.

He smiles for he has spoken
of the ancestors: his, ours.
We leave quietly, each alone,
knowing that they who come after us
and breaking
in these tides will find
red empty rooms
to measure long journeys.


## GRANDMOTHER: CROSSING JORDAN

Rippling hospital sheets
circle your brown body
and you sink
for the third time,
ready to rise alone
on the other side.

I reach out for you
and pull and pull
until your skin tears
from the bones of elbow,
arm, wrist, and fingers.

How it hangs empty,
loose. A glove
too large
for my hand.


## HEARTBEATS

Work out. Ten laps.
Chin ups. Look good.

Steam room. Dress warm.
Call home. Fresh air.

Eat right. Rest well.
Sweetheart. Safe sex.

Sore throat. Long flu.
Hard nodes. Beware.

Test blood. Count cells.
Reds thin. Whites low.

Dress warm. Eat well.
Short breath. Fatigue.

Night sweats. Dry cough.
Loose stools. Weight loss.

Get mad. Fight back.
Call home. Rest well.

Don't cry. Take charge.
No sex. Eat right.

Call home. Talk slow.
Chin up. No air.

Arms wide. Nodes hard.
Cough dry. Hold on.

Mouth wide. Drink this.
Breathe in. Breathe out.

No air. Breathe in.
Breathe in. No air.

Black out. White rooms.
Head hot. Feet cold.

No work. Eat right.
CAT scan. Chin up.

Breathe in. Breathe out.
No air. No air.

Thin blood. Sore lungs.
Mouth dry. Mind gone.

Six months? Three weeks?
Can't eat. No air.

Today? Tonight?
It waits. For me.

Sweet heart. Don't stop.
Breathe in. Breathe out.

■

# RITA DOVE

## (B. 1952)

*One of the most linguistically gifted poets of her (or any) generation, Rita Dove has at a young age amassed an impressive body of work, one that seems to deepen and assume more grandeur with each addition. Equally at home in brief, brittle lyrics or expansive narrative tales, Ms. Dove can also combine these modes, as in her Pulitzer Prize–winning* Thomas and Beulah, *into sequences of poems that tell whole stories (and histories) without sacrificing poetic imagery, insight, or technique. Her poems show the influences of her wide-ranging interests, from Sylvia Plath to the Austrian poet Georg Trakl to the blues, and involve subject matter as various as the visual artists Frida Kahlo and Albrecht Dürer and the intimate lives of poor blacks in factory-town Ohio. Rita Dove was born in Akron, Ohio, and was educated at Miami University and the University of Iowa. She is the author of four books of poems, a book of stories, and, most recently, a novel,* Through the Ivory Gate. *Currently Commonwealth Professor of English at the University of Virginia, she lives in Charlottesville. In May 1993, she was named Poet Laureate of the United States.*

## "TEACH US TO NUMBER OUR DAYS"

In the old neighborhood, each funeral parlor
is more elaborate than the last.
The alleys smell of cops, pistols bumping their thighs,
each chamber steeled with a slim blue bullet.

Low-rent balconies stacked to the sky.
A boy plays tic-tac-toe on a moon
crossed by TV antennae, dreams

he has swallowed a blue bean.
It takes root in his gut, sprouts
and twines upward, the vines curling
around the sockets and locking them shut.

And this sky, knotting like a dark tie?
The patroller, disinterested, holds all the beans.

August. The mums nod past, each a prickly heart on a sleeve.


## BEAUTY AND THE BEAST

Darling, the plates have been cleared away,
the servants are in their quarters.
What lies will we lie down with tonight?
The rabbit pounding in your heart, my

child legs, pale from a life of petticoats?
My father would not have had it otherwise
when he trudged the road home with our souvenirs.
You are so handsome it eats my heart away . . .

Beast, when you lay stupid with grief
at my feet, I was too young to see anything
die. Outside, the roses are folding
lip upon red lip. I miss my sisters—

they are standing before their clouded mirrors.
Gray animals are circling under the windows.
Sisters, don't you see what will snatch you up—
the expected, the handsome, the one who needs us?

# BANNEKER

What did he do except lie
under a pear tree, wrapped in
a great cloak, and meditate
on the heavenly bodies?
*Venerable,* the good people of Baltimore
whispered, shocked and more than
a little afraid. After all it was said
he took to strong drink.
Why else would he stay out
under the stars all night
and why hadn't he married?

But who would want him! Neither
Ethiopian nor English, neither
lucky nor crazy, a capacious bird
humming as he penned in his mind
another enflamed letter
to President Jefferson—he imagined
the reply, polite and rhetorical.
Those who had been to Philadelphia
reported the statue
of Benjamin Franklin
before the library

his very size and likeness.
A wife? No, thank you.
At dawn he milked
the cows, then went inside
and put on a pot to stew
while he slept. The clock
he whittled as a boy
still ran. Neighbors
woke him up
with warm bread and quilts.
At nightfall he took out
his rifle—a white-maned
figure stalking the darkened
breast of the Union—and
shot at the stars, and by chance
one went out. Had he killed?

*I assure thee, my dear Sir!*
Lowering his eyes to fields
sweet with the rot of spring, he could see
a government's domed city
rising from the morass and spreading
in a spiral of lights. . . .


## TOU WAN SPEAKS TO HER HUSBAND, LIU SHENG

I will build you a house
of limited chambers
but it shall last
forever: four rooms
hewn in the side of stone
for you, my
only conqueror.

In the south room all
you will need for the journey
—a chariot, a
dozen horses—
opposite,

a figurine household
poised in servitude
and two bronze jugs, worth more
than a family pays in taxes
for the privilege to stay
alive, a year, together . . .

but you're bored.
Straight ahead then, the hall
leading to you, my
constant
emperor. Here
when the stench of your
own diminishing
drives you to air (but

you will find none), here
an incense burner
in the form of the mountain
around you, where hunters pursue
the sacred animal
and the peaks are drenched
in sun.

For those times
in your niche when darkness
oppresses, I will set you
a lamp. (And a statue
of the palace girl you most
frequently coveted.)

And for your body,
two thousand jade wafers
with gold thread puzzled
to a brilliant envelope,
a suit to keep
the shape of your death—

when you are long light and clouds
over the earth, just as the legends prophesy.

## PARSLEY*

1. *The Cane Fields*

There is a parrot imitating spring
in the palace, its feathers parsley green.
Out of the swamp the cane appears

to haunt us, and we cut it down. El General
searches for a word; he is all the world
there is. Like a parrot imitating spring,

*On October 2, 1957, Rafael Trujillo (1891–1961), dictator of the Dominican Republic, ordered 20,000 blacks killed because they could not pronounce the letter r in *perejil*, the Spanish word for parsley.

we lie down screaming as rain punches through
and we come up green. We cannot speak an R—
out of the swamp, the cane appears

and then the mountain we call in whispers *Katalina*.
The children gnaw their teeth to arrowheads.
There is a parrot imitating spring.

El General has found his word: *perejil*.
Who says it, lives. He laughs, teeth shining
out of the swamp. The cane appears

in our dreams, lashed by wind and streaming.
And we lie down. For every drop of blood
there is a parrot imitating spring.
Out of the swamp the cane appears.

### 2. *The Palace*

The word the general's chosen is parsley.
It is fall, when thoughts turn
to love and death; the general thinks
of his mother, how she died in the fall
and he planted her walking cane at the grave
and it flowered, each spring solidly forming
four-star blossoms. The general

pulls on his boots, he stomps to
her room in the palace, the one without
curtains, the one with a parrot
in a brass ring. As he paces he wonders
Who can I kill today. And for a moment
the little knot of screams
is still. The parrot, who has traveled

all the way from Australia in an ivory
cage, is, coy as a widow, practising
spring. Ever since the morning
his mother collapsed in the kitchen
while baking skull-shaped candies
for the Day of the Dead, the general
has hated sweets. He orders pastries
brought up for the bird; they arrive

dusted with sugar on a bed of lace.
The knot in his throat starts to twitch;
he sees his boots the first day in battle
splashed with mud and urine
as a soldier falls at his feet amazed—
how stupid he looked!—at the sound
of artillery. *I never thought it would sing*
the soldier said, and died. Now

the general sees the fields of sugar
cane, lashed by rain and streaming.
He sees his mother's smile, the teeth
gnawed to arrowheads. He hears
the Haitians sing without R's
as they swing the great machetes:
*Katalina*, they sing, *Katalina*,

*mi madle, mi amol en muelte.* God knows
his mother was no stupid woman; she
could roll an R like a queen. Even
a parrot can roll an R! In the bare room
the bright feathers arch in a parody
of greenery, as the last pale crumbs
disappear under the blackened tongue. Someone

calls out his name in a voice
so like his mother's, a startled tear
splashes the tip of his right boot.
*My mother, my love in death.*
The general remembers the tiny green sprigs
men of his village wore in their capes
to honor the birth of a son. He will
order many, this time, to be killed

for a single, beautiful word.

# THE EVENT

Ever since they'd left the Tennessee ridge
with nothing to boast of
but good looks and a mandolin,

the two Negroes leaning
on the rail of a riverboat
were inseparable: Lem plucked

to Thomas' silver falsetto.
But the night was hot and they were drunk.
They spat where the wheel

churned mud and moonlight,
they called to the tarantulas
down among the bananas

to come out and dance.
*You're so fine and mighty; let's see*
*what you can do,* said Thomas, pointing

to a tree-capped island.
Lem stripped, spoke easy: *Them's chestnuts,*
*I believe.* Dove

quick as a gasp. Thomas, dry
on deck, saw the green crown shake
as the island slipped

under, dissolved
in the thickening stream.
At his feet

a stinking circle of rags,
the half-shell mandolin.
Where the wheel turned the water

gently shirred.

# DUSTING

Every day a wilderness—no
shade in sight. Beulah
patient among knicknacks,
the solarium a rage
of light, a grainstorm
as her gray cloth brings
dark wood to life.

Under her hand scrolls
and crests gleam
darker still. What
was his name, that
silly boy at the fair with
the rifle booth? And his kiss and
the clear bowl with one bright
fish, rippling
wound!

Not Michael—
something finer. Each dust
stroke a deep breath and
the canary in bloom.
Wavery memory: home
from a dance, the front door
blown open and the parlor
in snow, she rushed
the bowl to the stove, watched
as the locket of ice
dissolved and he
swam free.

That was years before
Father gave her up
with her name, years before
her name grew to mean
Promise, then
Desert-in-Peace.
Long before the shadow and
sun's accomplice, the tree.

Maurice.

# WEATHERING OUT

She liked mornings the best—Thomas gone
to look for work, her coffee flushed with milk,

outside autumn trees blowsy and dripping.
Past the seventh month she couldn't see her feet

so she floated from room to room, houseshoes flapping,
navigating corners in wonder. When she leaned

against a door jamb to yawn, she disappeared entirely.

Last week they had taken a bus at dawn
to the new airdock. The hangar slid open in segments

and the zeppelin nosed forward in its silver envelope.
The man walked it out gingerly, like a poodle,

then tied it to a mast and went back inside.
Beulah felt just that large and placid, a lake;

she glistened from cocoa butter smoothed in
when Thomas returned every evening nearly

in tears. He'd lean an ear on her belly
and say: *Little fellow's really talking,*

though to her it was more the *pok-pok-pok*
of a fingernail tapping a thick cream lampshade.

Sometimes during the night she woke and found him
asleep there and the child sleeping, too.

The coffee was good but too little. Outside
everything shivered in tinfoil—only the clover

between the cobblestones hung stubbornly on,
green as an afterthought. . . .

## THE GREAT PALACES OF VERSAILLES

*Nothing nastier than a white person!*
She mutters as she irons alterations
in the backroom of Charlotte's Dress Shoppe.
The steam rising from a cranberry wool
comes alive with perspiration
and stale Evening of Paris.
*Swamp she born from, swamp*
*she swallow, swamp she got to sink again.*

The iron shoves gently
into a gusset, waits until
the puckers bloom away. Beyond
the curtain, the white girls are all
wearing shoulder pads to make their faces
delicate. That laugh would be Autumn,
tossing her hair in imitation of Bacall.

Beulah had read in the library
how French ladies at court would tuck
their fans in a sleeve
and walk in the gardens for air. Swaying
among lilies, lifting shy layers of silk,
they dropped excrement as daintily
as handkerchieves. Against all rules

she had saved the lining from a botched coat
to face last year's gray skirt. She knows
whenever she lifts a knee
she flashes crimson. That seems legitimate;
but in the book she had read
how the *cavaliere* amused themselves
wearing powder and perfume and spraying
yellow borders knee-high on the stucco
of the *Orangerie.*

A hanger clatters
in the front of the shoppe.
Beulah remembers how
even Autumn could lean into a settee
with her ankles crossed, sighing
*I need a man who'll protect me*
while smoking her cigarette down to the very end.


## FLASH CARDS

In math I was the whiz kid, keeper
of oranges and apples. *What you don't understand,
master,* my father said; the faster
I answered, the faster they came.

I could see one bud on the teacher's geranium,
one clear bee sputtering at the wet pane.
The tulip trees always dragged after heavy rain
so I tucked my head as my boots slapped home.

My father put up his feet after work
and relaxed with a highball and *The Life of Lincoln.*
After supper we drilled and I climbed the dark

before sleep, before a thin voice hissed
numbers as I spun on a wheel. I had to guess.
*Ten,* I kept saying, *I'm only ten.*


## TURNING THIRTY, I
## CONTEMPLATE STUDENTS
## BICYCLING HOME

This is the weather of change
and clear light. This is
weather on its B side,
askew, that propels
the legs of young men
in tight jeans wheeling

through the tired, wise
spring. Crickets too
awake in choirs
out of sight, although
I imagine we see
the same thing
and for a long way.

This, then, weather
to start over.
Evening rustles
her skirts of sulky
organza. Skin
prickles, defining
what is and shall not be. . . .

How private
the complaint of these
green hills.


## CANARY

*for Michael S. Harper*

Billie Holiday's burned voice
had as many shadows as lights,
a mournful candelabra against a sleek piano,
the gardenia her signature under that ruined face.

(Now you're cooking, drummer to bass,
magic spoon, magic needle.
Take all day if you have to
with your mirror and your bracelet of song.)

Fact is, the invention of women under siege
has been to sharpen love in the service of myth.

If you can't be free, be a mystery.

## THE MUSICIAN TALKS ABOUT "PROCESS"

(after Anthony "Spoons" Pough)

I learned the spoons from
my grandfather, who was blind.
Every day he'd go into the woods
'cause that was his thing.
He met all kinds of creatures,
birds and squirrels,
and while he was feeding them
he'd play the spoons,
and after they finished
they'd stay and listen.

When I go into Philly
on a Saturday night,
I don't need nothing but
my spoons and the music.
Laid out on my knees
they look so quiet,
but when I pick them up
I can play to anything:
a dripping faucet,
a tambourine,
fish shining in a creek.

A funny thing:
when my grandfather died,
every creature sang.
And when the men went out
to get him, they kept singing.
They sung for two days,
all the birds, all the animals.
That's when I left the south.

# THE PASSAGE
(Corporal Orval E. Peyton
372nd Infantry, 93rd Division, A.E.J.)

*Saturday, March 30, 1918*

                    Got up
this morning at 2:45, breakfast at 3:30,
a beautiful sky, warm, and the moon bright.
I slept in my clothes, overcoat and socks.
I was restless last night, listening to the others
moving about.

Now, all the boys seem cheerful.
This will be a day never to be forgotten.
After breakfast—beef stew and coffee—
Charlie and I cleaned up the rest of the mail.

                 *

It is now 4:30 in the afternoon.
The whistle has blown for us
and everybody ordered down off deck.

I am not worried: I am anxious to go.

This morning we left camp at 7 and marched
silently along the town's perimeter to port.
No cheering nor tears shed, no one
to see us off, to kiss and cry over.
F Company was leading. I looked back at
several hundred men
marching toward they knew not what.
When we passed through the lower end of the city
a few colored people
stood along the street, watching.
One lady raised her apron to wipe away a tear.

I turned my head to see how the fellow next to me,
Corporal Crawford from Massachusetts,
was taking it. Our eyes met and we both smiled.

Not that we thought it was funny, but—
we were soldiers.
There were more things in this world
than a woman's tears.

*     *     *

*March 31*

                  Easter Sunday.
I was up to services held by a chaplain
but am not feeling well enough to get something to eat.
All the boys are gathered around the hatch
singing "My Little Girl." Talked to a sailor
who's been across twice; he says this ship
has had four battles with subs, each time
beating them off.

This boat is named *The Susquehanna*—
German built, interned before
the U.S. declared war. Her old name was *The Rhine.*
The other ship that left Newport News with us
was known as *Prinz Friedrich.*

We pulled out last night at 5
and I soon went to bed, so tired
I nearly suffocated, for I had left off my fan.
(We sleep in bunks three high and two
side by side with no ventilation
in quarters situated near the steam room.
The stair straight down. Everything in steel.)

*     *     *

*April 1 (All Fools Day)*

                  Nothing but water.
Just back from breakfast, home-style:
sausage, potatoes and gravy, oatmeal, coffee, bread
and an apple. The food seems better here than
in camp. Our boys do not complain much.

The sailors say we are the jolliest bunch of fellows
they have ever taken across. This boat's been over
twice before and according to them
this trip is the charm—either
the ship will be sunk or it will be good for the war.
I guess we are bound to have trouble, for it is said
the submarines are busy in this kind of weather.

Last night I could not eat all my supper, so went on deck.
No moon out but the sky full of stars,
and I remember thinking
*The future will always be with me.*
About 7 o'clock I saw a few lights some distance ahead
a little to the left. The boat made toward them;
as we drew nearer I recognized a red beacon.
Our gunners got busy and trained the sights.

We passed within 500 yards.
The stern was all lit. Someone said
it was a hospital ship.

*     *     *

*April 2, Tuesday*

                    Good breakfast—
bacon, eggs, grits, and of course coffee.
We ran into ships ahead about an hour ago.
I can see four, probably the rest of the fleet.

Most of the boys are on deck. A few are down here
playing blackjack and poker, and the band's playing, too.
I've been on deck all morning, up on a beam
trying to read the semaphore.

5:30 p.m. Just had supper. We ate with F Company
tonight: potatoes, corned beef, apple butter and coffee.
We've overtaken the other ships; I can see four more
to our ports. I got wet on deck about an hour ago.

I can hear the waves splashing! I think
I'll go up and smoke before it gets dark.

*     *     *

*April 3, Wednesday*

                    Just came down
off deck; the sea is high and waves all over.
I put on my rain coat to get in them—great sport!
There were six ships to our ports and a battleship starboard.

4 p.m. The storm is rocking us so,
the sides of the boat are touching the water.
No one can stay on deck without getting soaked.
I have been in my bunk all afternoon.

Quite a few of us are sick by now.
I feel a trifle dizzy;
there's something wrong with the ship,
I don't know what it is, but they called for
all the pipe fitters they could find.
Some of the boys have put on life preservers
but most don't seem to be afraid and are as jolly
as if they were on shore. Some say
they don't think we'll make it.
We are some kind of circus down here.

                    *

7 p.m.: our ship gets a wireless every evening
telling us the war news. Ever since supper
there has been a bunch on deck laughing,
singing, and dancing. A large wave swept
over the planks and drenched us all but
the stronger the sea, the more noise we made.
At last, just as Pickney had finished
a mock speech with "I thank you, ladies and gentlemen,"
a larger wave poured a foot of water on deck.

The sailors had crowded around us; they say
pity the Germans when a bunch like us hit them.

                    *    *    *

*April 4, Thursday*

Fifth day out.
I'm feeling all right—that is,
I don't feel like I did when I was on land,
but I am not sick. Last night I couldn't go to sleep
for a long while in that hot hole.
About 4 a.m., I put on my slippers
and went up for a breath of air.
The storm had passed and stars were shining,
half a dozen sailors busy with ropes.
One of the guards instructed me to close
my slicker, for my white underclothes were glowing.

Everybody this morning was in good spirits
and the deck was crowded with our boys.
Calm sea, a fair breeze blowing.
At ten o'clock we had "Abandon Ship" drill:
we were ordered below to our bunks
to put on life preservers, then
a whistle blew, some petty officers yelled
"all hands abandon ship," and we went
quickly to our places on the raft.
There are twenty-five of us in a boat.
My boat's number one.

*

When I think that I am a thousand miles
from land, in the middle of the Ocean,
I am not a bit impressed as I imagined I would be.
Things have certainly changed. A year ago
I was sitting in school, studying.
I had never been out of the state of Ohio
and never gone from home for more than
two weeks at a time. Now I'm away
eight months—four in the Deep South,
four in Virginia and now
on the High Seas.
I wonder where I'll be this time next year.

*    *    *

*April 5, Friday*

                                Last night after dinner
I started reading a book borrowed from Crawford
titled *Life of the Immortal.* Stopped
long enough for supper, and finished it
about an hour ago. Then with Shelton,
Davis, and Crawford, talked about literature.
I didn't get to bed before 10 o'clock
and did not feel like getting up this morning.

It is very hard to obtain soap on board
that will lather in salt water.
I can't get my hands clean without soap; but
one of the sailors gave me a piece
that's pretty good. So far I have managed
to stay fresh but some of the dudes don't care
and their hands are awful looking.
I haven't shaved since I've been
on board; I won't shave
until land is in sight.

                    *       *       *

*April 6, Saturday*

                                Wrestling match
with Casey; I was wet with sweat when we stopped
and went on deck to cool off.
We're served just two meals a day now, 9 and 3 o'clock.
Rich Tuggle and others bought a lot of cakes and candy
from the canteen, so I was too full to eat supper.

This morning in the mess line
Rick spotted some kind of large fish near our boat.
All I saw was its tail, but it shot up water
like I've seen in pictures in school.
*A whale,* I said, pointing, *it's a whale!*
But it went under without a noise.

                    *       *       *

*April 7, Sunday*

We had a death
on board last night, a cook by the name of Bibbie.
Chaplain Nelson held the service
on the other end of the boat.
Mess call sounded before he had finished.
(Pork, potatoes, corn and coffee.)

This is an ideal Sunday afternoon;
I wonder what we would be doing back home
if I was there. Now I will read a while
and then lie down. I am tired of the voyage.
I suppose there are lonesome days before me,
but no more so than those that have already passed.
I can make myself contented.
We are having very good weather.

It must have been a whale!

■

# THYLIAS MOSS

## (B. 1954)

*The poems of Thylias Moss are startling, at their best, for their strange and original use of imagery and voice. Sometimes comic, often darkly resonant, the poems deal with contemporary subject matter, for example, the social problems of young black girls, with an oblique touch that is not pedantic or heavy-handed. The poems can have the terseness of Dickinson and Brooks, or the long relaxed lines of Ginsberg and C. K. Williams. In her best moments, like "A Reconsideration of the Blackbird," the poems have both. Thylias Moss grew up in Cleveland, Ohio, graduated from Oberlin College, and went to graduate school at the University of New Hampshire. She is the author of five books of poems, and her work has appeared several times in the* Best American Poetry *annuals. She lives in Massachusetts and is a teacher at Phillips Andover.*

# LESSONS FROM A MIRROR

Snow White was nude at her wedding, she's so white
the gown seemed to disappear when she put it on.

Put me beside her and the proximity is good
for a study of chiaroscuro, not much else.

Her name aggravates me most, as if I need to be told
what's white and what isn't.

Judging strictly by appearance there's a future for me
forever at her heels, a shadow's constant worship.

Is it fair for me to live that way, unable
to get off the ground?

Turning the tables isn't fair unless they keep turning.
Then there's the danger of Russian roulette

and my disadvantage: nothing falls from the sky
to name me.

I am the empty space where the tooth was, that my tongue
rushes to fill because I can't stand vacancies.

And it's not enough. The penis just fills another
gap. And it's not enough.

When you look at me,
know that more than white is missing.

## THE UNDERTAKER'S DAUGHTER
## FEELS NEGLECT

Tonight, a beautiful redhead
whose hair he's combed six times.
It is always the same. He never finds
his way to my room. My mother played dead
the night I was conceived.
Like him I'm attracted
to things that can't run away from me.
I spit-shine aluminum pans.

It's been years since the mailman came, years
since I woke in the middle of the night
thinking a party was going on downstairs,
thinking my father was a magician
and all those scantily clad women his assistants,
wondering why no one could hear me,
why I was made to disappear permanently in the box.
I seldom wake at all anymore.


## A RECONSIDERATION OF THE BLACKBIRD

Let's call him *Jim Crow.*

Let's call him *Nigger* and see if he rises
faster than when we say *abracadabra.*

*Guess who's coming to dinner?*
Score ten points if you said blackbird.
Score twenty points if you were more specific, as in the first line.

What do you find *from here to eternity?*
Blackbirds.

*Who never sang for my father?*
The blackbirds who came, one after the other, landed on the roof
and pressed it down, burying us alive.
Why didn't we jump out the windows? Didn't we have enough time?
We were outnumbered (13 on the clothesline, 4 & 20 in the pie).
We were holding hands and hugging like never before.
You could say the blackbirds did us a favor.

Let's not say that however. Instead let the crows speak.
Let them use their tongues or forfeit them.

Problem: What would we do with 13 little black tongues?

Solution: Give them away. Hold them for ransom. Make belts.
Little nooses for little necks.

Problem: The little nooses fit only fingers.

Solution: Get married.

Problem: No one's in love with the blackbirds.

Solution: Paint them white, call them visions, everyone will want
    one.


## LANDSCAPE WITH SAXOPHONIST

The usual is there,
nondescript trees opened like umbrellas,
pessimists always expecting rain,
chickadees whose folding and unfolding wings
suggest the shuffling and reshuffling
of the cardsharp's deck;
nothing noteworthy except the beginning saxophonist
blowing with the efficacy of wolves addicted to pigs,
blowing down those poorly built houses,
the leaves off the trees, the water in
another direction, the ace of spades
into the ground with the cardsharp's bad intentions.
The discord and stridency set off landslides
and avalanches; his playing moves the earth
not lovers who are satisfied too quickly
and by the wrong things.

# CORNELIUS EADY

*The poems of Cornelius Eady convey the vagaries of human emotion with ease and are as likely to leave the reader touched with melancholy as doubled over in sidesplitting laughter. For example, Mr. Eady has written a line describing black life on Chicago's South Side as, among other things, a "rent party above the slaughter-house"; the two extremes of that image of urban life bracket his abilities as well. Unafraid of humor or sadness, he is already a master at composing and selecting the exactly right phrase, and of weaving those phrases into larger structures of verbal music and meaning. The origins of his sense of playfulness can be seen in his love of the work of Nicanor Parra and Thelonious Monk, whom he cites as influences along with Michael S. Harper, Lucille Clifton, Amiri Baraka, William Carlos Williams, and Walt Whitman. Cornelius Eady was born in Rochester, New York, is a graduate of Empire State College, and attended the MFA program at Warren Wilson College. He is a professor at the State University of New York at Stony Brook, and lives in New York City.*

## APRIL

Suddenly, the legs want a different sort of work.
This is because the eyes look out the window
And the sight is filled with hope.
This is because the eyes look out the window

And the street looks a fraction better than
    the day before.
This is what the eyes tell the legs,
Whose joints become smeared with a fresh sap
Which would bud if attached to a different limb.

The legs want a different sort of work.
This is because the ears hear what they've been
    waiting for,
Which cannot be described in words,
But makes the heart beat faster, as if
One had just found money in the street.

296 ■ EVERY SHUT EYE AIN'T ASLEEP

The legs want to put on a show for the entire world.
The legs want to reclaim their gracefulness.
This is because the nose at last finds the right scent
And tugs the protesting body onto the dance floor.
This is because the hands, stretching out in boredom,
Accidentally brush against the skirts of the world.


## RADIO

There is the woman
Who will not listen
To music. There is the man
Who dreams of kissing the lips
Attached to the voice.
There is the singer
Who reinvents the world
In musical notation.
There is the young couple
Who dance slowly on the sidewalk,
As if the rest of the street
Didn't exist.
There is the school boy
Whose one possession
Is an electric box
That scrambles the neighborhood.
There is the young girl
Who locks her bedroom door,
And lip-syncs in the mirror.
There is the young beau
Who believes in the songs so much,
He hears them
Even when
He isn't kissing someone.
There is the mother
Who absent-mindedly sways to the beat,
But fears the implications
For her daughter.
There is the man
Who carries one in his
Breast pocket
And pretends it's a Luger.

There are the two young punks
Who lug one into our car
On the stalled D train,
Who, as we tense for the assault,
Tune in a classical music station,
As if this were Saturday night
On another world.

## JACK JOHNSON DOES THE EAGLE ROCK

Perhaps he left the newspaper stand that morning
      dazed, a few pennies lighter,
The illustration of the crippled ocean liner
      with the berth he had the money
But not the skin to buy
Engraving itself
On that portion of the mind reserved for
      lucky breaks.
Perhaps the newsboy, a figure too small to
      bring back,
Actually heard his laugh,
As the *S.S. Titanic*, sans one prize fighter,
Goes down again all over New York,
Watched his body dance
As his arms lift the ship, now a simple millimeter thick,
      above his head
In the bustling air, lift it up
As though it was meant to happen.

## CROWS IN A STRONG WIND

Off go the crows from the roof.
The crows can't hold on.
They might as well
Be perched on an oil slick.

Such an awkward dance,
These gentlemen
In their spotted-black coats.
Such a tipsy dance,

As if they didn't know where they were.
Such a humorous dance,
As they try to set things right,
As the wind reduces them.

Such a sorrowful dance.
How embarrassing is love
When it goes wrong

In front of everyone.


## LEADBELLY

You can actually hear it in his voice:
Sometimes the only way to discuss it
Is to grip a guitar as if it were
Somebody's throat
And pluck. If there were

A ship off of this planet,
An ark where the blues could show
Its other face,

A street where you could walk,
Just walk without dogged air at
Your heels, at your back, don't
You think he'd choose it?
Meanwhile, here's the tune:
Bad luck, empty pockets,
Trouble walking your way
With his tin ear.

## INSOMNIA

You'll never sleep tonight.
Trains will betray you, cars confess
Their destinations,

Whether you like it
Or not.

They want more
Than to be in
Your dreams.

They want to tell you
A story.

They yammer all night and then
The birds take over,
Jeering as only
The well-rested can.


## SONG

*Nigger-Lover* is a song, spat out
Of an open car window
At dusk,

At the great mall in
Lynchburg, VA, the
First time in

Five years we've
Heard it. We
Almost made it,

Amazed this hasn't
Happened before. It
Was the end of

Our going away party.
We were walking out
Across the lot. What

Those drunken boys in
The black Chevy saw
Was so obvious. What

Else could they make
Of this invitation?
We almost made it,

Always carried the possibility
With us for years.
But it was

The end of our
Going away party. Almost,
Almost, almost got out

Scot-free, almost
Didn't have
To hear it

Right where
You are supposed
To hear it, almost

Didn't have to drive home
Thinking hard about
The headlights

At our backs, carry
Their hard singing
Away in our

Cars, in our heads. We
Almost, almost,
Almost

Got away. We were just
Walking out, soft
Twilight

In the hills surrounding
The lot, laughing
Our plump laughs,

Nearly gone.

## MUDDY WATERS & THE
## CHICAGO BLUES

Good news from the windy city: Thomas Edison's
Time on the planet has been validated. The guitars
And harps begin their slow translation
Of the street, an S.O.S. of what you need
And what you have. The way this life
Tries to roar you down, you have to fight

Fire with fire: the amplified power
Of a hip rotating in an upstairs flat
Vs. the old indignities; the static
Heat of *nothing, nowhere,*

*No how* against this conversation
Of fingers and tongues, this
Rent party above the
Slaughter-house.

■

# REUBEN JACKSON
## (B. 1956)

*Born in Augusta, Georgia, Reuben Jackson was educated at Goddard
College and the University of the District of Columbia. His poems are
urbane, thoughtful, delicate, and humorous, sometimes wistful or
even melancholic, which puts Mr. Jackson in the company of the art-
ists he cites as favorites and influences: William Carlos Williams,
Frank O'Hara, Amiri Baraka, and Marvin Gaye. Reuben Jackson lives
with his family in Washington, D.C.*

## for duke ellington

music is your mistress;
demanding constant love
and international settings.

as always, you stroll beside her.

aging, grumpy orchestra
springs into elegance at the drop
of your hand.

even so, there are casualties.

the years pass,
you bury rabbit and swee'pea,
run your fingers across the black keys,
dip the color in your hair.

cancerous nodes
rush toward a harrowing cadenza,
pen kisses paper.

a lover
in no particular hurry,
the music reveals itself
a negligee black note at a time.


## thelonious

bizarre?
mysterioso?

i say no.

for he swung like branches in march wind,

reached down
into the warm pocket of tenderness.

"little rootie tootie"
makes me dance a fat soft-shoe,

"monk's mood"
makes me sail.

but no bizarre,
no mysterioso.

he tilled song
like it was earth,

and he
a gardener
hell bent
on raising

any beauty
waiting
on the other
side.


## 63rd and broadway

my hotel room's small.
no space
for leaves
that swirl
above the idle
fountains of
lincoln center.

who's the statue
in the nearby
park?

(its benches lined
with chronic
shadows.)

a block away
is the church
where billie holiday's
funeral was held,

and farther west,
the lower case skyline
of new jersey.

gazing across the hudson,
i don't think of landfills,
jimmy hoffa,
or bruce springsteen,

but thelonious monk's last
exile:

standing on nica's
balcony in "catville"—

resisting the piano's advances,

and the city where i am happiest
alone.

# ELIZABETH ALEXANDER

## (B. 1962)

*Elizabeth Alexander was born in New York City and grew up in Washington, D.C. Educated at Yale, Boston University, and the University of Pennsylvania, she published her first book,* The Venus Hottentot, *in 1990, and currently teaches at the University of Chicago. Her poems demonstrate an acute preoccupation with the past, public and private, and often assume the form of dramatic monologues, with historical black personages relating emotions and experiences that may have been unexpected or even unsought, but that ring uncannily true.*

# THE VENUS HOTTENTOT
(1825)

    1. CUVIER

Science, science, science!
Everything is beautiful

blown up beneath my glass.
Colors dazzle insect wings.

A drop of water swirls
like marble. Ordinary

crumbs become stalactites
set in perfect angles

of geometry I'd thought
impossible. Few will

ever see what I see
through this microscope.

Cranial measurements
crowd my notebook pages,

and I am moving closer,
close to how these numbers

signify aspects of
national character.

Her genitalia
will float inside a labeled

pickling jar in the Musée
de l'Homme on a shelf

above Broca's brain:
"The Venus Hottentot."

Elegant facts await me.
Small things in this world are mine.

2.

There is unexpected sun today
in London, and the clouds that
most days sift into this cage
where I am working have dispersed.
I am a black cutout against
a captive blue sky, pivoting
nude so the paying audience
can view my naked buttocks.

I am called "Venus Hottentot."
I left Capetown with a promise
of revenue: half the profits
and my passage home: A boon!
Master's brother proposed the trip;
the magistrate granted me leave.
I would return to my family
a duchess, with watered-silk

dresses and money to grow food,
rouge and powders in glass pots,
silver scissors, a lorgnette,
voile and tulle instead of flax,
cerulean blue instead
of indigo. My brother would
devour sugar-studded non-
pareils, pale taffy, damask plums.

That was years ago. London's
circuses are florid and filthy,
swarming with cabbage-smelling
citizens who stare and query,
"Is it muscle? bone? or fat?"
My neighbor to the left is
The Sapient Pig, "The Only
Scholar of His Race." He plays

at cards, tells time and fortunes
by scraping his hooves. Behind
me is Prince Kar-mi, who arches
like a rubber tree and stares back
at the crowd from under the crook
of his knee. A professional
animal trainer shouts my cues.
There are singing mice here.

"The Ball of Duchess DuBarry":
In the engraving I lurch
toward the *belles dames,* mad-eyed, and
they swoon. Men in capes and pince-nez
shield them. Tassels dance at my hips.
In this newspaper lithograph
my buttocks are shown swollen
and luminous as a planet.

Monsieur Cuvier investigates
between my legs, poking, prodding,
sure of his hypothesis.
I half expect him to pull silk
scarves from inside me, paper poppies,
then a rabbit! He complains
at my scent and does not think
I comprehend, but I speak

English. I speak Dutch. I speak
a little French as well, and
languages Monsieur Cuvier
will never know have names.
Now I am bitter and now
I am sick. I eat brown bread,
drink rancid broth. I miss good sun,
miss Mother's *sadza.* My stomach

is frequently queasy from mutton
chops, the pale potatoes, blood sausage.
I was certain that this would be
better than farm life. I am
the family entrepreneur!
But there are hours in every day
to conjure my imaginary
daughters, in banana skirts

and ostrich-feather fans.
Since my own genitals are public
I have made other parts private.
In my silence I possess
mouth, larynx, brain, in a single
gesture. I rub my hair
with lanolin, and pose in profile
like a painted Nubian

archer, imagining gold leaf
woven through my hair, and diamonds.
Observe the wordless Odalisque.
I have not forgotten my Xhosa
clicks. My flexible tongue
and healthy mouth bewilder
this man with his rotting teeth.
If he were to let me rise up

from this table, I'd spirit
his knives and cut out his black heart,
seal it with science fluid inside
a bell jar, place it on a low
shelf in a white man's museum
so the whole world could see
it was shriveled and hard,
geometric, deformed, unnatural.

## NARRATIVE: ALI
a poem in twelve rounds

*Narrative*

1.

My head so big
they had to pry
me out.   I'm sorry
Bird (is what I call
my mother).   Cassius
Marcellus Clay,
Muhammad Ali;
you can say
my name in any
language, any
continent:   Ali.

2.

Two photographs
of Emmett Till,
born my year,
on my birthday.
One, he's smiling,
happy, and the other one
is after.   His mother
did the bold thing,
kept the casket open,
made the thousands look upon
his bulging eyes,
his twisted neck,
her lynched black boy.
I couldn't sleep
for thinking,
Emmett Till.

One day I went
down to the train tracks,
found some iron
shoe-shine rests
and planted them
between the ties

and waited
for a train to come,
and watched the train
derail, and ran,
and after that
I slept at night.

3.

I need to train
around people,
hear them talk,
talk back.    I need
to hear the traffic,
see people in
the barbershop,
people getting
shoeshines, talking,
hear them talk,
talk back.

4.

Bottom line:    Olympic gold
can't buy a black man
a Louisville hamburger
in nineteen-sixty.

Wasn't even real gold.
I watched the river
drag the ribbon down,
red, white, and blue.

5.

Laying on the bed,
praying for a wife,
in walk Sonji Roi.

Pretty little shape.
Do you like
chop suey?

Can I wash your hair
underneath
that wig?

Lay on the bed,
Girl.   Lie
with me.

Shake to the east,
to the north,
south, west—

but remember,
remember, I need
a Muslim wife.   So

Quit using lipstick.
Quit your boogaloo.
Cover up your knees

like a Muslim
wife, religion,
religion, a Muslim

wife.   Eleven
months with Sonji,
first woman I loved.

        6.

There's not
too many days
that pass that I
don't think
of how it started,
but I know
no Great White Hope
can beat
a true black champ.
Jerry Quarry
could have been
a movie star,
a millionaire,
a Senator,
a President—
he only had
to do one thing,
is whip me,
but he can't.

### 7. *Dressing Room Visitor*

He opened
up his shirt:
"KKK" cut
in his chest.
He dropped
his trousers:
latticed scars
where testicles
should be.   His face
bewildered, frozen,
in the Alabama woods
that night in 1966
when they left him
for dead, his testicles
in a Dixie cup.
You a warning,
they told him,
to smart-mouth,
sassy-acting niggers,
meaning niggers
still alive,
meaning any nigger,
meaning niggers
like me.

### 8. *Training*

Unsweetened grapefruit juice
will melt my stomach down.
Don't drive if you can walk,
don't walk if you can run.
I add a mile each day
and run in eight-pound boots.

My knuckles sometimes burst
the glove.   I let dead skin
build up, and then I peel it,
let it scar, so I don't bleed
as much.   My bones
absorb the shock.

I train in three-minute
spurts, like rounds:    three
rounds big bag, three speed
bag, three jump rope, one
minute breaks,
no more, no less.

Am I too old?    Eat only
kosher meat.    Eat cabbage,
carrots, beets, and watch
the weight come down:
two-thirty, two-twenty,
two-ten, two-oh-nine.

9.

Will I go
like Kid Paret,
a fractured
skull, a ten-day
sleep, dreaming
alligators, pork-
chops, saxophones,
slow grinds, funk,
fishbowls, lightbulbs,
bats, typewriters,
tuning forks, funk,
clocks, red rubber
ball, what you see
in that lifetime
knockout minute
on the cusp?
You could be
let go,
you could be
snatched back.

10. *Rumble in the Jungle*

*Ali boma ye,*
*Ali boma ye,*
means kill him, Ali,
which is different
from a whupping

which is what I give,
but I lead them chanting
anyway, *Ali
boma ye,* because
here in Africa
black people fly
planes and run countries.

I'm still making up
for the foolishness
I said when I was
Clay from Louisville,
where I learned Africans
lived naked in straw
huts eating tiger meat,
grunting and grinning,
swinging from vines,
pounding their chests—

I pound my chest but of my own accord.

11.

I said to Joe Frazier,
first thing, get a good house
in case you get crippled
so you and your family
can sleep somewhere.    Always
keep one good Cadillac.
And watch how you dress
with that cowboy hat,
pink suits, white shoes—
that's how pimps dress,
or kids, and you a champ,
or wish you were, 'cause
I can whip you in the ring
or whip you in the street.
Now back to clothes,
wear dark clothes, suits,
black suits, like you the best
at what you do, like you
President of the World.
Dress like that.
Put them yellow pants away.

We dinosaurs gotta
look good, gotta sound
good, gotta be good,
the greatest, that's what
I told Joe Frazier,
and he said to me,
we both bad niggers.
We don't do no crawlin'.

12.

They called me "the fistic pariah."

They said I didn't love my country,
called me a race-hater, called me out
of my name, waited for me
to come out on a streetcar, shot at me,
hexed me, cursed me, wished me
all manner of ill-will,
told me I was finished.

*Here I am,*
like the song says,
*come and take me,*

"The People's Champ,"

myself,
Muhammad.

# SELECTED BIBLIOGRAPHIES
# AND AUTHOR INDEX

To Disembark (1981)
Blacks (1987)

*Other*

Maud Martha, A Novel (1953)
Bronzeville Boys and Girls (1956)
A Broadside Treasury [anthology]
   (1971)
The World of Gwendolyn Brooks
   (1971)
Report from Part One (1972)
The Tiger Who Wore White Gloves:
   or, What You Are You Are (1974)

**LUCILLE CLIFTON** 150

*Poems*

Good News About the Earth (1972)
An Ordinary Woman (1974)
Two-Headed Woman (1980)
Good Woman: Poems and a Mem-
   oir, 1969–1980 (1987)
Next: New Poems (1987)
Quilting (1991)

*Other*

Some of the Days of Everett Ander-
   son [children] (1970)
The Boy Who Didn't Believe in
   Spring [children] (1973)
Generations: A Memoir (1976)
Three Wishes (1976)
Everett Anderson's Goodbye (1983)

**JAYNE CORTEZ** 160

*Poems*

Pissstained Stairs and The Monkey
   Man's Wares (1969)
Festivals and Funerals (1971)
Scarifications (1973)
Mouth on Paper (1977)
Coagulations: New and Selected
   (1984)
Poetic Magnetic (1991)

**RALPH DICKEY** 222

*Poems*

Leaving Eden (1975)

**MELVIN DIXON** 268

*Poems*

Change of Territory (1983)

*Other*

Ride Out the Wilderness: Geog-
   raphy and Identity in Afro-
   American Literature (1987)
Trouble the Water [novel] (1989)
Red Leaves, Vanishing Rooms
   [novel] (1990)

**RITA DOVE** 272

*Poems*

The Yellow House on the Corner
   (1980)
Museum (1983)
Thomas and Beulah (1986)
Grace Notes (1989)

*Other*

Fifth Sunday [stories] (1985)
Through the Ivory Gate [novel]
   (1992)

**CORNELIUS EADY** 296

*Poems*

Kartunes (1980)
Victims of the Latest Dance Craze
   (1986)
The Gathering of My Name (1991)

**MARI EVANS** 62

*Poems*

I Am a Black Woman (1970)
Nightstar, 1973–1978 (1981)

# ACKNOWLEDGMENTS

The editors gratefully acknowledge the following for permission to reprint material:

AI. "Cuba, 1962" from *Cruelty* by Ai. Copyright © 1970, 1973 by Ai. Reprinted by permission of Houghton Mifflin Co. All rights reserved; "Riot Act, April 29, 1992," "Self Defense," and "Endangered Species" from *Greed* by Ai. Copyright © 1993 by Ai. Reprinted by permission of W. W. Norton & Company, Inc.

ELIZABETH ALEXANDER. "The Venus Hottentot" from *The Venus Hottentot* by Elizabeth Alexander. Copyright © 1990 by Elizabeth Alexander. Reprinted by permission of the University Press of Virginia; "Narrative: Ali." Copyright © by Elizabeth Alexander. Reprinted by permission of the author.

IMAMU AMIRI BARAKA. "Preface to a Twenty Volume Suicide Note," "Each Morning," "Three Modes of History and Culture," and "Clay" from *Selected Poetry* by Imamu Amiri Baraka. Copyright © 1961, 1979 by Amiri Baraka; "Black Art" and "Black Bourgeoisie" from *Black Magic* by Amiri Baraka. Copyright © 1969 by Amiri Baraka; "Short Speech to My Friends" from *The Dead Lecturer* by Amiri Baraka. Copyright © 1964. Reprinted by permission of Sterling Lord Literistic, Inc.

GEORGE BARLOW. "A Dream of the Ring: The Great Jack Johnson" from *Soledad* by George Barlow; "In My Father's House." Copyright © by George Barlow. Reprinted by permission of the author.

GERALD BARRAX. "Last Letter," "King: April 4, 1968," and "The Singer" from *An Audience of One* by Gerald Barrax. Copyright © 1980 by Gerald Barrax. Reprinted by permission of The University of Georgia Press.

GWENDOLYN BROOKS. "The Mother," "of DeWitt Williams on his way to Lincoln Cemetery," "Piano after War," "Mentors," "Beverly Hills, Chicago," "The Bean Eaters," "We Real Cool," "A Bronzeville Mother Loiters In Mississippi. Meanwhile, a Mississippi Mother Burns Bacon," "The Last Quatrain of the Ballad of Emmett Till," "The Lovers of the Poor," "Boy Breaking Glass," "Medgar Evers," "The Blackstone Rangers," and "The Near-Johannesburg Boy" from *Blacks* by Gwendolyn Brooks; "A Song in the Front Yard," "Sadie and Maud," and excerpts from "Winnie" and "Children Coming Home" by Gwendolyn Brooks; "To an Old Black Woman Homeless and Indistinct" first appeared in Eugene Redmond's 1993 *"Drumvoices Revue."* All poems copyrighted by Gwendolyn Brooks and reprinted by permission of the author.

sion of Graywolf Press, Saint Paul, Minnesota; "A Sorrow Since Sitting Bull." Copyright © by Christopher Gilbert. Reprinted by permission of the author. MICHAEL S. HARPER. "Double Elegy," "In Hayden's Collage," "The Drowning of the Facts of a Life," and "The Loon" from *Healing Song for the Inner Ear* by Michael Harper. Reprinted by permission of the University of Illinois Press; "For Bud," "Remember Mexico," "American History," "Here Where Coltrane Is," "Last Affair: Bessie's Blues Song," "Homage to the New World," "Nightmare Begins Responsibility," "Grandfather," "Tongue-Tied in Black and White," and "Eve (Rachel)" from *Images of Kin* by Michael Harper. Reprinted by permission of the University of Illinois Press; "Studs." Copyright © Michael S. Harper. Reprinted by permission of the author.

ROBERT HAYDEN. "A Ballad of Remembrance," "The Ballad of Sue Ellen Westerfield," "Homage to the Empress of the Blues," "Those Winter Sundays," "Runagate Runagate," "Frederick Douglass," "The Dream," "El-Hajj Malik El-Shabazz," "October," "A Plague of Starlings," "The Night-Blooming Cereus," "Free Fantasia: Tiger Flowers," "A Letter from Phillis Wheatley," "Crispus Attucks," "Paul Laurence Dunbar," "Ice Storm," "The Point," "The Islands," "Astronauts," and "[American Journal]" from *Collected Poems of Robert Hayden* edited by Frederick Glaysher. Copyright © 1985 by Erma Hayden. Reprinted by permission of Liveright Publishing Corporation.

REUBEN JACKSON. "for duke ellington," "thelonious," and "63rd and broadway" by Reuben Jackson. Copyright © by Reuben Jackson. Reprinted by permission of the author.

DOLORES KENDRICK. "Jenny in Love," "Sophie, Climbing the Stairs," "Jenny in Sleep," and "Sadie Snuffs a Candle" from *The Women of Plums: Poems in the Voices of Slave Women* by Dolores Kendrick. Copyright © 1989 by Dolores Kendrick. Reprinted by permission of the author.

ETHERIDGE KNIGHT. "Hard Rock Returns to Prison from the Hospital for the Criminal Insane," "The Idea of Ancestry," "Haiku," "For Freckle-Faced Gerald," " A Poem for Black Relocation Centers," and "Dark Prophecy: I Sing of Shine" from *The Essential Etheridge Knight* by Etheridge Knight. Copyright © 1986 by Etheridge Knight. Reprinted by permission of the University of Pittsburgh Press.

YUSEF KOMUNYAKAA. "Untitled Blues" and "Elegy for Thelonius" from *Copacetic* by Yusef Komunyakaa. Copyright © 1984 by Yusef Komunyakaa; "Fragging," "Between Days," and "Facing It" from *Dien Cai Dau* by Yusef Komunyakaa. Copyright © 1988 by Yusef Komunyakaa; "How I See Things" from *I Apologize for the Eyes in My Head* by Yusef Komunyakaa. Copyright © 1986 by Yusef Komunyakaa. All reprinted by permission of the University Press of New England. "February in Sydney" from *New and Selected Poems: Neon Vernacular.* Copyright © 1989 by Yusef Komunyakaa. "Euphony" first appeared in *The Iowa Review* (Vol. 22, No. 3, 1992). Reprinted by permission of the author.

AUDRE LORDE. "Beams" and "For the Record" from *Our Dead Behind Us, Poems by Audre Lorde.* Copyright © 1986 by Audre Lorde; "Coal," "Prologue," and "Father Son and Holy Ghost" from *Undersong, Chosen Poems*

*ment* by Derek Walcott. Copyright © 1987 by Derek Walcott. Reprinted by permission of Farrar, Straus & Giroux, Inc.

MARILYN NELSON WANIEK. "Freeman Field," "Three Men in a Tent," "Lonely Eagles," "Star-Fix," "Porter," and "Tuskegee Airfield" from *The Homeplace* by Marilyn Nelson Waniek. Copyright © 1990 by Marilyn Nelson Waniek; "My Grandfather Walks in the Woods" and "Emily Dickinson's Defunct" from *For the Body* by Marilyn Nelson Waniek. Copyright © 1978. Reprinted by permission of Louisiana State University Press.

SHERLEY ANN WILLIAMS. "Letters from a New England Negro" from *Some One Sweet Angel Chile* by Sherley Anne Williams. Copyright © 1982 by Sherley Anne Williams. Reprinted by permission of the author.

JAY WRIGHT. "The White Deer" from *Boleros* by Jay Wright. Copyright © 1988 by Jay Wright; "An Invitation to Madison County," "The Albuquerque Graveyard," "Love in the Weather's Bells," and "Meta-A and the A of Absolutes" from *Selected Poems* by Jay Wright. Copyright © 1987 by Jay Wright. Reprinted by permission of Princeton University Press; "The Lake in Central Park," "Madrid," and "Desire's Persistence" from *Elaine's Book* by Jay Wright. Copyright © 1986 by Jay Wright; "Death as History," "Compassion's Bird," and "Don José Gorostiza Encounters el Cordobés." Copyright © by Jay Wright. Reprinted by permission of the author.

AL YOUNG. "Dance of the Infidels," "Detroit 1958," "How the Rainbow Works," "Lester Leaps In," and "The Blues Don't Change" from *Heaven: Collected Poems, 1958–1988* by Al Young. Copyright © 1966, 1969, 1978, 1982 by Al Young; "How Stars Start," "Jazz As Was," "From Bowling Green," and "Leaving Syracuse." Copyright © 1992 by Al Young. Reprinted by permission of the author.